D0314104

CONCRETE
DESIGN

CANCELLED

Return to

This book i
below. Ple
telephone

27 JUL

27 NOV 20

10 JI

25 AP.

b JU

CONCRETE DESIGN

SARAH GAVENTA

MITCHELL BEAZLEY

in association with

 **Blue Circle**

CONCRETE DESIGN

BY SARAH GAVENTA

First published in Great Britain in 2001 by Mitchell Beazley,
an imprint of Octopus Publishing Group Ltd,
2–4 Heron Quays, Docklands, London E14 4JP

First published in paperback in 2006

Copyright © Octopus Publishing Group Ltd 2001

All rights reserved. No part of this work may be reproduced or utilized
in any form or by any means, electronic or mechanical, including
photocopying, recording or in any information storage and retrieval
system, without the prior permission of the publisher.

ISBN 1 84533 183 4

A CIP catalogue record for this book is available from the British Library.

Set in Frutiger, Orator, OCRB and Trade Gothic

Produced by Toppan Printing Co., (HK) Ltd
Printed and bound in China

Commissioning Editor **Mark Fletcher**
Art Directors **Vivienne Brar** and **Geoff Borin**
Project Editors **Emily Asquith** and **Hannah Barnes-Murphy**
Designer **Amzie Viladot**
Editor **Jonathan Hilton**
Production **Catherine Lay** and **Alex Wiltshire**
Picture Researcher **Geri May**
Proofreader **Jane Donovan**
Indexer **Ann Parry**

DUNDEE CITY COUNCIL

LOCATION
SCIENCE AND BUSINESS

ACCESSION NUMBER
C00 431 200X.

SUPPLIER
HOLT

PRICE
£6.99

CLASS No.
721.0445

DATE
12/5/06

CONTENTS

FOREWORD PIERS GOUGH

Concrete is a very capable material, and it is spectacularly important in architecture. Though loved by architects, what was done in Britain in the 1960s has put the public off, and it has since needed new champions to restore it to favour. Many architects have kept their heads down, always speaking up for great concrete projects such as The National Theatre and The Barbican in London, but wary about working in the material on a similar scale. But, a lot of 1960s precast concrete buildings were noxious, inhuman in attitude, and carelessly disregarded human needs for texture and scale. A sample of concrete when it appears in the architect's office can look interesting and charming, but quite scary when you see it on a massive scale.

Telling planners you want to build in concrete still scares them. One can't deny that stained concrete is very nasty indeed, and if the formwork isn't correct it can be very risky. I use concrete in its jelly formed, precast state for sculptural details, such as spiral columns, and I certainly prefer concrete for framed buildings instead. But I probably haven't built enough, or on a large enough scale in concrete, so I feel quite guilty about it as a construction material. Perhaps there is a lack of courage in Britain; we need the confidence and the contractors to build in concrete in the way architects do in Europe, particularly France, where it is their material of choice. In France you can pick up a modular shuttering system at any builders' merchant. Perhaps it is also because of the climate that concrete works better there, after all concrete France is really Southern France. There are actually some good concrete bridges in Britain, even on our motorways, but concrete still looks best, from the outside, in Mediterranean countries.

One successful concrete project in the UK, however, is the Jubilee Line extension of the London Underground system, where concrete was used to create one of the most important architectural projects in the country. The marvellous massive interiors evoke the sense of being outdoors.

The use of concrete in interiors is a fashion trend, but a very nice one as concrete is an emotional material and extremely expressive. It can be as smooth as a cashmere jacket or as rough as hell. Concrete is undoubtedly respectable as an architectural material and is very sensual. But concrete has an ugly side, which, perversely, is another reason why architects like it.

In the UK at the turn of the 21st century, there persists a kind of "bunker"-like design mentality and, although some architects are still thrilled by bunker buildings, I'm not. This approach isn't seen in North or South America, where freedom and freshness has been celebrated, creating some of the most sensuous concrete buildings in the world, such as the work of Eero Saarineen and Oscar Niemeyer. In South America, concrete is sexy, like the culture. In Britain and Northern Europe, the material is intellectual but cold. I like the work of Santiago Calatrava; his concrete undercrofts of railway stations such as Lisbon are delicious and magnificent. He is redressing the balance, reacting against a time when every bridge was a box. I also love the work of architects such as Will Bruder who produces "get off on this" concrete architecture, big and bold like the cowboy country where he practices. There they think big. And of course, John Lautner is the king. He understood that concrete is sloppy, you should let it go. Don't make it vertical and straight and don't attempt to constrain its possibilities. Why make concrete imitate other materials? Let the material speak about its capabilities. Otherwise it is like trying to put jelly into a rectangular mould. What a waste.

INTRODUCTION

Just how important is a construction material such as concrete? Considered a dirty word by the vast majority of the public, the material has become synonymous with the words "shoddy", "cheap" – even "inhuman". And, when you look at some of the decaying tower blocks of the Gorbals and Easterhouse in Glasgow, it is difficult to disagree.

What would be wrong, though, would be to blame these social housing disasters on the material itself, rather than on the planning philosophy adopted at the time; a philosophy that was quick to house people in ghettos that had been built quickly and shoddily, using unproven construction systems, and then subjected to inadequate maintenance and slow decay. It is high time that concrete was forgiven and rehabilitated, especially now that the international design community is beginning to experiment more and more with the new techniques and ideas surrounding this ancient material. Concrete isn't going to disappear; it is one of the few viable materials for the future of our built environment – now is the time to examine all the possibilities of concrete, and to use it with flair and imagination.

Finally, concrete is coming in from the cold and entering our domestic world. Prior to the recent fashion for minimalism, it had not been widely perceived as a suitable material for the domestic environment and this, combined with the recent enthusiasm for the loft aesthetic, means it is now seen more frequently, though in a predominantly clean, fair-faced finish.

Concrete isn't a cheap building material – in fact, well-crafted concrete can be very expensive – but it is a more environmentally sustainable construction material than, for the sake of argument, natural stone or wood. It can be restored, repolished, and revarnished and, if well maintained, concrete can last for hundreds, if not thousands of years.

This book, though not intended to be a guide to the history of concrete in design and architecture, is an attempt to examine designers' relationships with the material; to look at the qualities that the material possesses and, hopefully, to spark a wider interest in its use. This is not to suggest that all interiors should be made entirely of concrete – indeed, the material is perhaps most successful when used in combination with others. But what is

→ PANTHEON

The Pantheon, Rome (AD 127). Detail of the light-weight concrete dome in which crushed pumice was used as an aggregate. It is one of the few buildings to survive intact after the decline of the Roman Empire. With a diameter of over 43 metres (141 feet) it is a testament to the durability of concrete (and the skill of Roman engineers) and was the largest dome in the world until the 20th century.

↑ PROPHET SAMUEL

The Prophet Samuel in Infancy (*c*.1850). One of the earliest examples of a concrete statuette thought to have been made by James Aspdin, the elder son of the inventor of Portland cement.

apparent is that the full potential of concrete has yet to be realized, and that some of the techniques developed in the 1960s and 70s, predominantly for exterior use, have now been lost, leaving only an apparently limited, contemporary repertoire of possibilities open to the architect and designer.

The importance of concrete in the evolution of architectural history is obvious to the architectural profession – to such an extent that it barely warrants a mention in their writings. Architects who have been on pilgrimages to Marseilles to visit Le Corbusier's famous Unité d'Habitation; who admire the work of Tadao Ando, Louis Kahn, or Carlo Scarpa, accept the material as the basic component of contemporary architecture. But it is a younger generation of architects who are looking at the work of the 1960s and 70s with fresh eyes and some distance, and these are the designers who are really pushing at the boundaries of design in concrete .

To design successfully in concrete is to understand the material from a structural point of view. And those architects who love it, understand it, and experiment with it, work closely with engineers to develop their designs. It is no surprise, then, that some of the most startling, if not architecturally coherent, projects have been produced either by architects and designers with an engineering background, such as Santiago Calatrava, Pier Luigi Nervi, and Felix Candela – or those who admire their work, such as Oscar Niemeyer and John Lautner.

Designers of furniture, homewares, and even jewellery, often have a different approach and set of references to architects. This is particularly noticeable in their attitudes toward concrete. Many designers engage with the material far more directly and intimately than an architect would, in an attempt to make small-scale work from a typically large-scale material. In the hands of the designer, concrete can become a fashion item, reflecting current lifestyle trends in a way that architecture, with its longer-term view and timescales, often cannot. Hence, this book is intended to show both the breadth and scale of concrete design, useful for the general reader who may still need convincing that concrete is a sensuous, high-quality material to be admired and respected.

In Monty Python's film, *Life of Brian*, John Cleese asks his assembled rebels "What have the Romans ever done for us?" The one thing they forgot to include in the rather long list of achievements that followed, was the invention of concrete; the Romans' "greatest architectural legacy", according to the architectural historian Sir John Summerson.

There is evidence to suggest that earlier cultures, including the Ancient Egyptians, had discovered their own limited forms of concrete. But it was in the second century BC that the Romans quarried pink, sand-like material from Pozzuoli, Italy. Initially mistaken for sand, this fine, volcanic ash contained silica and

← BAZLEY-WHITE HOUSE
The first all-concrete house in Swansombe,
Kent (1835). Practically everything is built of
concrete – walls, tiles, window frames, and
decorative work – even the garden gnomes.

← MILLARD HOUSE

Millard House, Pasadena (1923). In the Millard House, Frank Lloyd Wright uses concrete block construction, in combination with clambering foliage, to great monumental and textural effect.

→ TANNER HOUSE

An advertisement for Red Triangle Portland Cements, with the concrete house built for Douglas Tanner, Esq., designed by Tanner and Horsburgh, Birmingham, UK. Red Triangle attempted to equate concrete, in the mind of the consumer, with hygiene, middle class comfort, and dependability.

alumina, which combine chemically with lime to produce what became known as pozzolanic cement. One of the first large-scale uses of the material was in the theatre at Pompeii, constructed in 75 BC. Concrete was predominantly used for the foundations and as an infill material because, it needed reinforcement to give it tensile strength, which was otherwise poor. Attempts were made to reinforce concrete with bronze, but this was only partially successful, because bronze has a higher co-efficient of thermal expansion than concrete (unlike steel), which causes the concrete to crack.

Throughout the Roman empire, local raw materials were used to make concrete. Relatively lightweight aggregates, such as pumice stone, were also added to the mix, which explains the name of the material, from the Roman word *concretus*, meaning "grown together" or "compounded". Such lightweight concretes were used in some of the arches of the Coliseum, and also in the dome of

the Pantheon in Rome – the domed, concrete roof of which is testimony to the durability of the material.

Hadrian's Wall (125–30 AD), in the north of England, was constructed with a core of stone bonded together with concrete. Over a period of some 800 years, the Romans had developed concrete from crude filler to major structural material. All this was to change, however, with the decline of the Roman Empire, which also signalled a slump in the engineering and structural development of the material. Many of the important structural and engineering discoveries were temporarily lost during the Middle Ages, and concrete enjoyed only very limited use as an infill or load-bearing material for foundations, such as for the spire of Salisbury Cathedral in Wiltshire – the tallest spire in the UK.

A revival of interest in concrete occurred in the middle of the 18th century in Europe, as part of the scientific and entrepreneurial

Concrete House built for Douglas Tanner, Esq.

Architects: Tanner and Horsburgh, Birmingham.
XVII

MODERN LIVING CONDITIONS

demand a higher standard of Hygiene, Comfort, and Labour Saving.

CONCRETE HOUSES

meet these requirements.

Here is an excellent example of the clever use of concrete in modern house construction inaugurating a new era of dignified beauty in architecture and introducing a new standard of hygiene and comfort.

Such houses meet the demand of today and just as Red Triangle brands of Portland Cement are specified for dependability in Britain's newest and mightiest buildings, so can they be used with confidence in concrete house construction.

RED TRIANGLE PORTLAND CEMENTS

DEPENDABILITY

revolution. In 1756, John Smeaton, an engineer from Leeds, experimented with developing a cement superior to lime mortar – which had been used up until that time – for underwater use as the mortar for the new Eddystone lighthouse near Plymouth, off the Devon coast in the English Channel.

A major achievement in the history of concrete was brought about by Joseph Aspdin, who, in 1824, took out a patent for the manufacture of Portland cement – so called because, when set, it was thought to resemble Portland stone in colour. His cement was the most superior type of its day. Improved versions of Portland cement gradually replaced Roman cement in mortars and renders, but was not generally mixed with aggregates to make concrete for structural use until the mid-1800s.

The first all-concrete house was built for John Bazley-White, a manufacturer of Roman cement, at Swanscombe, Kent, in 1835. It had concrete walls, window frames, and decorative work – even concrete garden gnomes. However, the technology of reinforcement was not at that time suitably advanced to allow a concrete floor. Other houses built entirely from concrete followed the Bazley-White House, but not yet on a large scale. From the 1840s onwards, precast concrete tended to be more popular for details, such as paving, garden ornaments, and balustrading, rather than large-scale architectural elements. In 1875, William Lascelles patented a low-rise, precast-concrete housing system, but it was the development of steel reinforcement that really turned concrete into the most important modern construction material.

← AIRCRAFT HANGAR
Aircraft hangar at Orbetello, Italy (1939).
The precast frame, shown before the erection
of the cladding, is a shining sculptural feat
by the great Italian architect/engineer Pier
Luigi Nervi. Nervi was a major influence
on architects such as John Lautner and
Oscar Niemeyer, who overcame his fear of
flying to visit Nervi in Italy. He made possible
the seemingly impossible expressive forms for
which these architects are so renowned.

→ PENGUIN POOL
Concrete performs a double helix. The
Penguin Pool at London Zoo, UK (1934) by Berthold
Lubetkin (who, in 1932 established the architec-
tural practice Tecton). One of the best-loved
Modernist buildings in the UK. Overnight it brought
Modernism to Britain and demonstrated a new
aesthetic of reinforced concrete.

The existence of reinforced concrete has been documented from as early as 1830, and throughout the 19th century it was known by many names, including ferro-concrete.

In 1848, a French lawyer, Jean-Louis Lambot, built the world's first reinforced concrete boat. He plastered a layer of fine concrete or mortar over a network of iron rods and mesh to produce ferro-cement. The following year, the French engineer Joseph Monier made plant tubs of reinforced concrete, and fellow engineer François Coignet developed a special technique for encasing an iron skeleton framework in concrete.

William Wilkinson, a Newcastle-based builder, applied for a patent in 1854; the builder stated that the use of second-hand wire colliery rope could be embedded in fresh concrete, the ends formed into loops, or splayed by opening out the strands and twirling them in different directions, so that the rope could not be drawn out when the concrete was under load. Significantly, this appears to be the first time that reinforced concrete was considered as a composite structure, as opposed to metalwork simply encased in concrete. Not much seems to have come of this until François Hennebique and his company, Hennebique & Le Brun, developed a system of reinforcement. In 1898, he created the first multistorey, reinforced concrete-framed building in Britain – the Weavers' Mill in Swansea. His system was successful and became very popular. In 1901 it was used to build the first reinforced concrete bridge at Chewton Glen in the New Forest in Britain. Within ten years, around 40,000 different structures had been constructed using Hennebique's system.

Robert Malliart, a Swiss engineer and pupil of Hennebique, was influential in the field, due to his construction of the first concrete shell roof at the Gare de Bercy in Paris, in 1910. Further developments were made by another Frenchman, Eugène Freyssinet, who, seven years later, discovered the value of mechanical vibration for compacting concrete, and who pioneered the system of prestressing, which still bears his name.

By the 1890s, concrete was being used extensively for engineering projects, such as docks, riverbanks, and bridges, but not for "proper" architecture. It was the material's intrinsic qualities that were causing something of a moral dilemma. Concrete was

← UNITE D'HABITATION

Detail of the Unité d'Habitation in Marseilles, France (1945–52) by Le Corbusier. Le Corbusier's iconic image of the modulor man is impressed into the concrete. In his pre-war concrete work, Le Corbusier rendered over any roughness or imperfections; at the Unité and in his later work such as the government buildings at Chandigargh, India (1951–6), he left the surfaces raw to create a "rugged grandeur" and provided an important inspiration for many architects.

← UNITE D'HABITATION

Detail of external staircase and wall for the Unité d'Habitation. The wood strip shuttering of the staircase contrasts with the precast blocks of the wall to create a carefully considered pattern.

←↑ NOTRE DAME-DU-HAUT

Notre Dame-du-Haut, Ronchamp, France (1950–55). Le Corbusier presented his highly sculptural creation: "I give you this chapel of clear faithful concrete, shaped perhaps with temerity but certainly with courage, in the hope that it will seek art in you (as in those who will climb the hill) and echo of what we have drawn into it."

The huge roof is a shell of reinforced concrete protected by several coats of waterproofing. The repetitive linear pattern of the form work is clearly, and deliberately, visible on the under-side of the roof (see below right).

considered pagan (given its Roman heritage) and so unsuitable as a construction material for Gothic Revival Christian buildings. As it had no natural form of its own, concrete was viewed as a material lacking in moral fibre, without character, and, if used at all, it should be faced with a more "moral" material, such as stone. According to Peter Collins in his book *Concrete: The Vision of a New Architecture,* when "Victorians first learnt of concrete they were not so much intrigued by the limitless possibilities offered by its plastic potential, as intimidated by the unprincipled character of its fabrication, since such methods found no place in the annals of Christian architecture and had no precedents except in pagan buildings and text."

Concrete's lack of natural form confused architects in an age when, as Collins says, "No material was to be made to look like any other material." The safest bet was to hide away the ignoble concrete, an attitude that appeared to be justified by the fact that when the material was used, the outcome was often poor – cheap labour and badly designed form work were often to blame, but frequently overlooked as contributory factors. Or, better still, instead of disguising concrete, the material was left out of architecture altogether, and used only for building where such moral dilemmas did not arise. Since it was cheap and quick to build with, requiring little skilled labour, concrete soon became the official medium for industrial building.

So much technological progress was made in the construction industry in the 19th century, and so much effort was made to develop concrete, that any attempt to accredit discoveries and new techniques to individual nations becomes difficult. Simultaneous discoveries were taking place throughout Europe, especially in France and Britain. It was the Europeans, such as the Englishman Ernest L Ransome, who brought new techniques to America, however it wasn't until the end of the 19th century that some of the most impressive and boldest concrete structures were developed in the United States.

← CLIFTON CATHEDRAL
Clifton Cathedral, Bristol, UK (1973) by the Percy Thomas Partnership. Concrete became a material suitable for religious iconography with *The Stations Of The Cross* moulded concrete and fibreglass panels by William Mitchell. Originally, the panels were to be cast in situ, but because they could not be sufficiently protected during the reconstruction of the rest of the building, they were installed afterwards.

↑ CLIFTON CATHEDRAL

The theme of hexagonals and equilateral triangles
pervades the whole cathedral. The nearly white
reinforced concrete clearly bears the imprint of the
wooden shuttering. There is no paint, plaster, or
added colour, aside from simple furnishings.

↑ COVENTRY CATHEDRAL

Coventry Cathedral, Coventry, UK, (1956–62) by
Basil Spence. The nave canopy is supported by 14
elegantly tapered, prestressed precast columns
made with a light blue-grey concrete. Originally,
the interior was to be faced with pink stone but it
was decided that concrete would better set off the
stained glass windows by John Piper and others.

Ransome is the apparent inventor of the concrete frame in its American incarnation. In 1844, he left the Patent Concrete Stone Company in England, manufacturers of a form of concrete invented by his father, Frederick Ransome. In the late 1860s Ernest L Ransome travelled to the United States to introduce his father's invention to California. Ransome had developed patents for reinforced concrete using twisted bars set transversely to carry tensile stresses. However, in California this simple, and now standard, solution was met with very little enthusiasm. In spite of this, between 1886 and 1887 Ransome built the very first reinforced concrete bridges in North America in Golden Gate Park, San Francisco, which still stand today.

The *American Architect and Building News* wrote in 1900 that the advantages of concrete are: "first speedy construction, second low cost, third daylight illumination, fourth shockproofness, fifth maintenance economy, and sixth fireproofness." The architectural critic Peter Reyner Banham noted that other materials, such as steel, are capable of all of the above except "fireproofness", and indeed, it was a dramatic fire that brought about a conversion to concrete on a mass scale in building construction in the United States. As Banham recounts:

"In 1902 the East Coast plant of Pacific Coast Borax at Bayonne, New Jersey went up in a spectacular fire that attracted national attention because it was so hot that steel twisted and iron melted into shapeless puddles on the floor. But the floors survived and so did the internal columns and the external walls, which were all made of the same material, fireproof reinforced concrete. There could have been no more convincing demonstration of the virtues of the material."

The sheer scale and simplicity of the new concrete grain elevators, the factories, the water towers, and the industrial buildings were an inspiration to the Modern Movement, both in form and material.

In Europe it is Auguste Perret and his brother Gustave who are cited as the pioneers of reinforced concrete in the first decades of the 20th century. Originally trained as architects, they studied at the Ecole des Beaux Arts in Paris in the early 1890s, and worked as students in their father's successful building firm. After their father died in 1905, they took over the company, and actively began to build and design concrete-framed buildings as contractors and consultants for other architects. Auguste was also designing his first important work in his own right, the famous apartment block in the rue Franklin in Paris in 1903–4 – the first domestic use of a concrete frame. The turning point came in 1911, however, when the brothers – having been hired only as contractors – took over the high-profile commission to design the concrete-framed Theâtre des Champ-Elysées, ousting from the project the celebrated Belgian architect Henry van de Velde.

In 1908, Le Corbusier, the Swiss-born French architect, worked briefly in the Perret office, which may go some way towards explaining his later enthusiasm for reinforced concrete as "the building material of the future". Architect Bertold Lubetkin also

← DE LA WARR PAVILION
The Art Deco spiral staircase is perhaps the most famous architectural element of the De la Warr Pavilion, Bexhill, UK (1935) by Serge Chermayeff and Eric Mendelsohn.

→ DE LA WARR PAVILION

Exterior of the De la Warr Pavilion. The architects originally planned to use a reinforced concrete construction but eventually decided to use steel. Instead it is still assumed that this modernist landscape is, in fact, concrete. This Deco style became emblematic of British seaside architecture.

 → SALTDEAN LIDO

The more restrained Saltdean Lido in East Sussex, UK (1938) by R W H Jones, demonstrating the classic Modernist details of large windows and undulating form made possible by the use of steel and concrete. Its design was heavily influenced by the De la Warr Pavilion just along the coast.

studied in the Perret office in 1924, just after Perret had completed his masterpiece – the Church of Notre Dame du Raincy. Designed in 1922, it was a large church constructed within a very small budget, built from exposed concrete with pierced concrete screens and decoration. Working with Perret, Lubetkin learned about the potential of reinforced concrete, though he was to use the material in a far less restrained manner than his teacher.

In 1927 Lubetkin studied at the Ecole Superieur de Beton Armé, a private institution run by an engineer, where he learned more about the structural properties of the medium. His excellent education was put to good use when he came to England, joined the Tecton group, and built the Penguin Pool at London Zoo (1934) and Highpoint I and Highpoint II (1933–5). These, among numerous other projects, allowed Lubetkin a certain degree of experimentation. For the first time he rejected standard shuttering and developed his own construction system, which allowed him to lessen the amount of concrete used for each project.

By 1927 reinforced concrete was beginning to gain acceptance and recognition within the more progressive architectural circles. This was largely because some significant and influential texts were being published or were being prepared for publication. Paul Jamot's *A & G Perret et l'Architecture du Beton Armé* was published in France; Le Corbusier's *Vers Une Architecture* was translated into English. The eccentric Francis Onderdonk's *The Ferro Concrete Style* was being prepared in the United States, in which the author suggested that all those who were interested in concrete should adopt Esperanto as an international language to communicate and exchange ideas and developments. In addition, *Architectural Design in Concrete* by T P Bennet and F R Yerbury was published.

Concrete was not embraced quite so vigorously by all of the great Modernists – for Ludwig Mies van der Rohe, steel was the preferred material. In the catalogue for the immensely influential exhibition 'The International Style' (1931) by Henry-Russell Hitchcock and architect Philip Johnson, concrete is mentioned only in passing within a list of suitable "surfacing materials".

At this stage, concrete technology was still in its adolescence. Many projects built before the Second World War, which today we

← BRASILIA

The Cathedral in Brasilia (1959–70) by Oscar
Niemeyer. The construction of an entire capital
city in only two years and the design of such
expressive forms was only made possible by the
use of concrete. Le Corbusier said to Niemeyer,
"Oscar, in your eyes you always have the mountains
of Rio. With concrete you construct the baroque."

→ THE NATIONAL THEATRE

The National Theatre, London, UK (1967–76) by
Denys Lasdun. Viewed from Waterloo Bridge, the
"strata" and "tower" elements are clearly visible.
The form of the strata was inconceivable in any
other material than concrete. Lasdun always
planned for the concrete to remain unpainted and
left with a rough texture. For the terraces and fly
towers a pale grey in situ concrete was chosen to
match the stone of nearby Waterloo Bridge,
Somerset House and St Paul's Cathedral.

tend to assume were reinforced concrete buildings, were, in fact, steel-framed or even brick-built and covered in stucco in imitation of concrete. The Modernist De la Warr Pavilion by Erich Mendelsohn and Serge Chermayeff, though initially designed to be constructed from reinforced concrete, was in the end steel-framed – in fact, the first major welded steel-framed building in England – and the highly sculptural expressionist Einstein Tower, also by Erich Mendelsohn, was made of rendered brick. Architects such as Berthold Lubetkin, who had detailed structural knowledge of reinforced concrete, instead led the way.

Village and Town, one of a series of children's books published by Puffin in the 1930s, provides an insight into the hopes and aspirations invested in the material at the time, by predicting the kind of new world that concrete would help to build:

"This new way of building has given us ways of preventing towns spreading and creeping over the countryside. Tall blocks of flats have been built that house hundreds of people. The best ones have been built to look beautiful and to be convenient to live in. These buildings take up so little ground space that there is plenty of room for gardens and trees … Concrete is being used to build new, clean-looking individual houses, too … Proper use of reinforced concrete has made these buildings look very different from the old buildings, but they rely for their beauty on simple shapes and simple patterns made by the windows." A Modernist utopia, the failure of which has turned concrete into a scapegoat, and precipitated a public relations disaster from which the material has yet to fully recover.

After the Second World War, when mass reconstruction started to take place, steel was in short supply and so architects had little choice but to turn to reinforced and prestressed concrete. Le Corbusier had originally wanted to use steel for his Unité d'Habitation (1945–52), but due to the shortages of building materials he chose concrete instead, and, as a result, created one of the most influential and innovative concrete housing structures in the world. The Unité was constructed from prestressed concrete; and Reyner Banham noted that the concrete used was a rough and imprecise material, "a messy soup of suspended dusts, grits and sump aggregate, mixed and poured under conditions subject to

↑ GATWICK SOUND BARRIER
This new acoustic barrier (1999) at Gatwick airport is 430 metres long (1,411 ft) and constructed of curved, precast concrete panels. It helps to protect nearby residents from the noise created by aircraft using a new standing area.

→ LYONS TGV STATION
View of the platform area at the TGV station, Lyons (1989–94) by Santiago Calatrava. With his monumental forms, Calatrava makes innovative use of the plastic potential of concrete; his work combines art, architecture, and sculpture.

the weather and human fallibility." The building was one of the first examples of the rough naturalness of concrete being actively celebrated, with little disguising of, or apology for, marks and flaws inherent in the material.

The rapid reconstruction of houses, bridges factories, and schools destroyed during the war was the main challenge facing the construction industry in Britain, and skilled craftsman and structural materials were in short supply. In response to this, systems for building permanent low-rise housing from prefabricated reinforced concrete elements were quickly developed.

The explosion in the use of precast concrete in the early 1960s – and a subsequent proliferation of manuals and books on concrete techniques – resulted in the development of many industrialized building systems. Prefabricated wall, floor, and roof units were factory-produced and assembled on site with the minimum of labour and effort. With the urgent need to rebuild most of Europe's shattered cities after the war, it seemed to be the most logical method of construction and, by 1965, there were over two hundred systems available in Britain alone. Many of the systems were badly produced, inadequately tested in the country's hurry to build new homes, and often failed, resulting in the public's disillusionment with concrete, and the widespread assumption that it was a cheap and shoddy material.

Over the last ten years, things have changed. Concrete is once again the material of choice for designers, and a substantial amount of impressive concrete architecture has been built. Although the examples illustrated here are confined to the domestic, they demonstrate that leading architects – such as Tadao Ando, Herzog & de Meuron, Rem Koolhaas, and Denton Corker Marshall (DCM) – are once more exploring concrete as a medium. The work of the American Minimalist artist Donald Judd has also been an inspiration for contemporary designers. At his Chinati Foundation at Marfa, Texas, fifteen giant, hollow concrete rectangular prisms lie in the landscape like the shells of Minimalist apartments. And, if imitation really is the highest form of flattery, then the recent appearance of woollen carpet tiles printed to look like a concrete pavement, and wallpaper that mimics fair-faced concrete proves that concrete is once again back in favour.

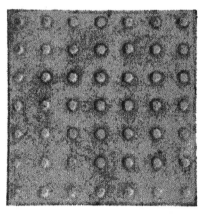

↑ CARPET TILES
The concrete paving-stone effect wool carpet tiles designed by Geraldine Heminway for Milliken demonstrate concrete's new fashionable status, reflecting the demand for the "look" but with a softer touch underfoot.

↓ WALLPAPER
The highest form of flattery is imitation. Here, concrete effect wallpaper substitutes for the real thing, instantly.

↑ CHINATI FOUNDATION

The influence of the work of Minimalist artist Donald Judd can be seen in the use of concrete in contemporary architecture and interior design. Here is an installation of hollow concrete monoliths ('15 Untitled Works in Concrete') at his Chinati Foundation, Marfa, Texas, USA (1980–84). Each piece measures 2.5 x 2.5 x 5 metres (8.2 x 8.2 x 16.4 ft) and is made from 25-cm (10-in) thick slabs.

STRENGTH

STRENGTH

Depending on how it is used, concrete can combine the tensile strength of steel with the compressive strength of stone. When concrete first emerged as a possible material for the construction of long-span structures, it was treated structurally in the same way as wood or steel. Since then, concrete's great strength has allowed it to be used for practically all types of major engineering projects, including the construction of lighthouses, high-rise buildings, roads, culverts, bridges, sea barriers, tunnels, and dams. Of all the bridges built in Britain since 1945, approximately 70 per cent of them have been made of concrete.

In architecture the strength of concrete has been exploited to create structures of a shape and scale never before seen. The expressionist works of the Spanish architect/engineer Santiago Calatrava are an awe-inspiring testament to the strength and beauty of concrete. The mighty concrete ribs spanning the railway station at Lyon airport in France, and the monolithic concrete vaults at Zurich station, emphasize in their colossal forms the properties of this material.

Only when it is reinforced is concrete really strong, however. If, for example, an unreinforced concrete beam is loaded at mid-span, the top compresses and the bottom is then in tension. Adding reinforcement overcomes this inherent weakness and thereby controls the material's tendency to crack.

It is the constituents of concrete that determine its strength. The calcareous materials used to make the cement (the chalk or limestone) provide the calcium. This is the substance that reacts with the silica, alumina, and iron in the argillaceous materials (the shale or clay) to form a clinker of calcium silicates, calcium aluminate, and calcium aluminoferrite. The cement clinker is then finely ground up with a small amount of gypsum to create what is known as Portland cement. It is the addition of water to the cement that causes it to set and harden. This occurs because of a chemical reaction between the water and the calcium silicates, which causes cement hydrates to grow and interlock with one another. Called hydration, this process can last for a long time, thus increasing the

← INDUSTRIAL SITE
Brangmyr Tyre Factory in Wales (1951), by the architects Co-Partnership and Ove Arup. The structure is remarkable for its 9 reinforced concrete shell domes spanning its production floor. The factory now lies derelict and under threat of demolition.

→ BRIDGE CONSTRUCTION
Santiago Calatrava's stunning Alamillo Bridge with its elegant concrete spine designed for the Seville Expo of 1992 in Spain.

strength of the concrete over a period of perhaps many months. Therefore the mix of the ingredients is fundamental to concrete's structural properties.

The proportion of water added to the concrete mix is critical in determining its permeability, as well as its strength and resistance to weather, wear and other destructive agencies. Too high a percentage of water dilutes the cement paste and weakens the adhesion between the particles, and results in a weak concrete. Concrete mixes are described in terms of the proportions of their constituent materials. The mix is specified according to the required strength, appearance, durability, and workability of the finished product. By altering the proportions of aggregates, cement, and water, changes can be made to the properties of both the fresh and hardened concrete.

A range of special properties can be imparted to the fresh concrete through the use of admixtures — accelerators to speed up the hardening process, for example, and retarders to slow it down. In some circumstances, plasticizers are also crucial additions to the mix, allowing it to flow well — for example, around steel-reinforcing ironwork — without the need to add any extra water, which would simply serve to undermine its strength. Air-entraining admixtures can be used to introduce small bubbles that help the hardened concrete resist the destructive contraction and expansion of the material brought about by freezing and thawing.

The versatility of concrete seems to defy all our preconceptions of the material. Simply by changing the type of aggregate used, concrete can be made so light that it can float on water, or made so heavy that it is almost twice its usual density. Concrete can be made totally impermeable to moisture for use in the construction of gigantic dams, or porous enough to be used in the making of filter-beds at sewage treatment plants, where water needs to percolate freely through as part of its whole cleansing and purification process.

About three-quarters by volume of concrete consists of a combination of fine and coarse aggregates — sand, gravel, and crushed rock — obtained from pits, quarries, and the seabed. In addition to these traditional aggregates, there are modern versions, such as pulverized fuel ash and expanded shale. Both of these are used to make lightweight aggregates. Recycling is even an option, and to reduce the impact that concrete production has on the environment, the crushed remains of demolished concrete structures can be reused as aggregate for new ones.

The inspirational work of the designers and architects featured in this chapter demonstrates both the strength and versatility of concrete, from the structural feats of John Lautner and the undomestic, monumental scale of Denton Corker Marshall, to the whole concrete shells of Koolhaas and Herzog & de Meuron. Strength is not usually an issue in the domestic environment, as the scale of the projects is too small for it to be of major concern. However, the architects are certainly utilizing concrete's quality of strength in order to create strong, visual statements invoking a sense of permanence, safety, and solidity.

→ UNDERGROUND DESIGN

The imposing concrete canopy of the Underground station at Canary Wharf in London's revitalized Docklands was designed by Norman Foster and Partners (1999) as part of the Jubilee Line extension programme, which involved the construction of a series of architect-designed, predominantly concrete, stations.

SHEATS/GOLDSTEIN HOUSE

USA | JOHN LAUTNER

John Lautner (1911–94) was the indisputed master of domestic concrete architecture in the USA. As a former pupil of Frank Lloyd Wright, with whom he studied at Taliesin for six years, Lautner was certainly familiar with Wright's use of ornamental concrete, but he elected to use the material in very different ways. Wright disapproved of using poured concrete because its free form meant that it had no intrinsic qualities of its own – it could literally become any shape. This, though, was exactly what Lautner loved about it.

Lautner set up in practice in Los Angeles, at first using wood for the majority of his houses, but gradually converting to the material that would make his futuristic dreams a reality – concrete. Though relatively unknown in Europe, his idiosyncratic work seems familiar, since many of his dramatic houses have appeared in films and commercials. The most obvious of these is the Elrod house, which, in the James Bond film "Diamonds are Forever", is where billionaire Willard White was held captive by the high-kicking Thumper and Bambi. So fantastic is the space that most people would have believed it to be another set designed by Ken Adams.

For Lautner, "Concrete is the very best material for withstanding sun, wind, fire, and time, and with it one can get a solid yet free, permanent and desirable space, formed and flowing to suit the specific needs of the client."

The Sheats/Goldstein House, one of Lautner's grandest and most magnificent projects, is a case in point. Designed originally in 1963, it was remodelled between 1980 and 1994, when Lautner designed the concrete furniture and fittings. The theme was crystalline, with irregular angles echoing and complementing those of the coffered concrete roof spanning the living area. Although the furniture was of concrete construction, upholstered leather cushions in warm browns were added for comfort and to enrich

→ BREAKFAST BAR

Echoing the design of the concrete-built furniture in the living room, this breakfast bar, with its concrete worktop, is a forerunner of the popular application of concrete seen today in commercial bars and kitchens.

the overall colour scheme. The house, in particular, demonstrates Lautner's admiration for the work of architects Eero Saarinen, Oscar Niemeyer, and the great architect/engineer Pier Luigi Nervi.

The most striking aspect of the house is its massive coffered concrete roof studded with glass tumblers to allow dappled light into the living room below. Later additions by Lautner were the long bank of concrete seating and the coffee tables, with a single pedestal supporting a thick sheet of glass. In the bedroom, the bed-base and headrest are also of concrete, and the material encases the sideboard and storage spaces in the dressing areas. In front of the bed, looking out over dramatic views across Los Angeles, is what is known in the USA as a "Lounge"– a day bed with a V-shaped concrete backrest where you can lie back, place your cocktail on the glass side table, slide back the glass walls, and gaze out at the view while enjoying the evening breezes. Here, concrete is used as a statement of pure, unadulterated luxury and decadence.

Perhaps the most beautiful feature is the washbasin, with its single tap (also designed by the architect). In contrast to the rather rough finish to most of the concrete, the washbasin is smooth and polished. Touches such as this, and the warm Bubinga wooden floors and doors, ensure that spaces appear warm and inviting.

In considering this commission alone, Lautner's reputation as the master of domestic concrete architecture in the USA is indisputable. At the Sheats/Goldstein House, as with all his projects, Lautner was continuing to experiment and invent, using techniques way ahead of the technologies of the time. Often misunderstood, and constantly battling with critics and the media, Lautner proved that concrete was a suitable material for the domestic interior more than 40 years before it was accepted, albeit rather grudgingly, into the contemporary interior design palette.

↑ BEDROOM

View of the concrete handbasin with its single tap, designed by Lautner. The contrast between the smooth finish of the sink top and the rougher concrete wall can be clearly seen..

→ LOUNGE

In this view of the living area, the leather-upholstered concrete banquettes can be seen. The dappled light is natural, coming from glass tumblers embedded in the massive coffered concrete ceiling.

BORDEAUX HOUSE FRANCE 1998 | REM KOOLHAAS/OMA

Rem Koolhaas, along with his architectural practice, the Office for Metropolitan Architecture based in Rotterdam, is one of the most important architects, writers, researchers, and teachers working today. As well as being an inspiration to a generation of students, he is also responsible for some of the most influential ideas in the field of urban planning and design, and has a incisive understanding of the dynamics of cities.

The Bordeaux House is an extraordinary design – one, however, that was born out of a terrible misfortune. The couple who commissioned the house were living in an old building in Bordeaux when the man was involved in a serious car accident. As a result, he was confined to a wheelchair, and the couple were then faced with the prospect of finding a new home suitable for their changed circumstances. Their prime requirement was for a house that would allow him the maximum possible freedom of movement. As he relayed to the architect in the early planning stages: "Contrary to what you would expect, I don't want a simple house. I want a complex house, because the house will define my world."

Rem Koolhaas's idea was to create three linked "houses", stacked one on top of each other. The bottom "house" would be half-submerged beneath the ground and contain all the communal and socializing areas, including the kitchen and dining space. Above this, the second "house" would be the most important, containing the main open living space. The first-floor walls are completely glazed allowing spectacular views of the city of Bordeaux in the distance. This storey was designed, as Koolhaas himself describes, as "a glass room – half inside, half outside – for living." Above the main living space would be the topmost and third "house", contrasting dramatically with the middle storey. Koolhaas created a concrete box, which is glazed on the side elevations, and which cantilevers out over the lower levels, to house the bedrooms and bathrooms.

One of the key features that makes these spaces work so well for a wheelchair user is the large internal elevator, a platform, measuring 3 x 3.5 m (10 x 11½ ft), running up the central core of the stack. Open on all sides, the platform fills the gap in the floor as it stops at each level, and the shaft in which it runs is lined on

↑ GLASS ROOM

In this view of the glass room, the elevator platform in the centre is rising up to join the level of the floor. The open space is designed to be, says the architect Rem Koolhaas, "half inside – half outside".

→ ELEVATOR SHAFT

The brilliance of the design concept can be appreciated in this view of the glass room. Now the elevator platform completes the bedroom level above, leaving the open shaft and the hydraulic ram visible.

one side by a three-storey bookshelf. Books, files, reference materi-al can all readily be selected as the elevator moves up or down. This gives the owner the all-important freedom to move about freely within his own home. As Koolhaas says: "The movement of the elevator continually changes the architecture of the house. A machine is its heart." Importantly, Koolhaas perceives the elevator as another room within the house; a room that can move to all of the storeys, or between them, and one that was particularly designed with the client in mind.

The use of concrete throughout the stack is on a major scale. Each "house" has a concrete floor and the exposed concrete ceilings reveal the structure of the building. And in the kitchen, even the worktop surfaces are made out of concrete.

In the children's bedroom at the top of the stack of "houses", a large, pivoting, circular panel has been cut out of the exterior concrete wall to allow more light and air to enter and, when seen from the outside, the aperture provides a visual focus for an otherwise plain façade. The same visual game is repeated in the wall of the courtyard next to the main façade. This recurring circular motif is echoed in the dramatic sweeping spiral ramp that provides access to the private lower storey of the house; and crops up again in the small circular windows that are punched out of the heavy concrete upper storey.

Throughout the house, concrete has been teamed with warm-toned woods, glass, perspex, and eclectic furniture to create a machine that feels more human than mechanical.

← BEDROOM
A circular, pivoting aperture allows additional light into the bedroom, situated at the top of the housing stack. The form of the aperture is echoed in the small windows cut out of the patio wall in the background.

→ USER'S PERSPECTIVE
From this viewpoint, looking up from the elevator room through the shaft to the skylight above, it is possible to appreciate the concrete construction methods in the underside of the floor, as well as being able to see just what a practical storage and access solution the book-lined shaft is for a wheelchair user.

SPIRAL STAIRCASE

UK 2001 | NICHOLAS HELM & MARIA SPEAKE

Retrouvius is an architectural reclamation and design business established by Maria Speake and Adam Hills in 1993, after the pair graduated from Glasgow School of Art in architecture. "Bridging the gap between destruction and construction is our philosophy," explains Speake. Helm Architects was established in 1992 and their experience with historical and listed buildings has given them an appreciation of traditional techniques and the way in which new and old methods can be brought together to bring about the restoration of residential and commercial buildings. In this project Nick Helm demonstrates how contemporary architecture and natural materials, such as concrete, can be combined in an original way.

Here, the brief was to bring the narrow living spaces of an early Victorian house into the 21st century. The dark and isolated basement and the ground floor bore no relationship to the garden, or to each other, and both spaces were depressing and unusable.

The addition of a new concrete staircase was pivotal to the design. It was installed at the back of the building where it could mediate between the different levels of garden and house, and placing it in the double height space with roof glazing above not only generated a link between the different levels, but also provided vertical movement through a very three-dimensional space.

Using concrete for a complex form such as the spiral staircase gave Speake and Helm the opportunity to experiment with the shifting relationship between form and function. Speake describes their thinking behind the project: "To be a usable sculpture, a solid, independent object in a robust, external material – a garden object brought inside – offered us a great opportunity for unusual expression. The use of concrete meant that the unstable-sounding rattling of a traditional metal spiral staircase was eliminated."

The construction was complicated, as Helm explains: "It required a large-scale architectural model so that it could be clearly understood and translated into three-dimensional computer drawings. The forms or moulds into which the concrete would be poured were factory-made, with a computer guiding a hot wire through solid cylinders of polystyrene." These cylinders took the place of the traditional timber shuttering, which would have been impossibly expensive. The surfaces were left raw and rough, since Speake felt that, "to tamper with them would be to smooth away the story".

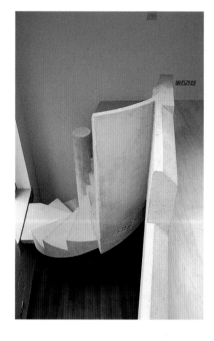
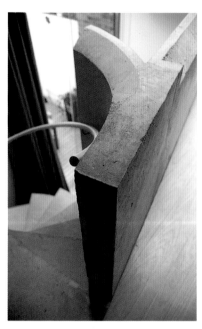

↑ ↓ STAIRCASE
The concrete spiral treads of the staircase fan out around the central concrete core to create a sculptural and very solid staircase.

→ FROM THE GARDEN

A view of the staircase as seen from the garden, showing the glass doors and dining room on the rehabilitated ground-floor level.

BEYER HOUSE

USA 1975–83 | JOHN LAUTNER

Once it was complete, this far from traditional beach house, perched high among cliffs on a rocky outcrop in Malibu, California, USA, became the client's permanent residence.

"The design has an arched roof, tilted toward the ocean. This not only protects the house from the setting sun in the west, it also helps to direct both the view and the space outward, toward the magnificent ocean. The undulating, freely cut roof edge suits the dramatic setting of sky, rocks, and waves. This has created a very free and totally ungeometric flowing space for living in intimacy and harmony with the ocean and the site. Additional boulders were brought in to be used as part of the house and its furnishing. Indeed, much of the furniture and cabinetwork are built from concrete, joining boulders together, including the shell for the water bed in the master bedroom. Stone and concrete flooring has been used to complete the beach-house environment," wrote the house's architect, John Lautner.

The project was compromised to some degree by certain planning difficulties and budget constraints – it took eight years, for example, to obtain all the planning permissions necessary for the project to proceed. It also had to be replanned to conform to tighter budget constraints – and keeping projects within budget was not one of Lautner's strengths. In light of this, the original plan for a concrete roof was changed to one made from wood and plaster. The idea behind the design of the house was to capture the spirit of the waves and surf at its feet, demonstrated in the building's curves and sweeping forms. Outside comes inside, not only in the layout, but also through the use of boulders and stone that blur the boundaries between the interior and exterior landscapes.

It is the use of concrete that pulls all the elements together and links all the other materials, playing more of a background role to the more dramatic flagstones and rocks. But no other material could have brought coherence to this design, making the disparate elements come together to create a home that is part rock pool, part cave. The dappled sunlight employed by Lautner gives the impression of light diffused through water, which heightens the rock-pool effect.

This project amply demonstrates that concrete does not have to dominate in order to be effective. Even when it is used in collaboration with other dramatic materials it still holds its own, providing visual relief from the more eye-catching elements.

→ LIVING ROOM
A view of Lautner's "free and totally ungeometric flowing space for living in", with its mix of materials – including natural rocks, flagstones, and a concrete fireplace. The eye is inexorably drawn to the carefully framed sea view.

RAWLINGS HOUSE | USA 1980 | JOHN LAUTNER

On a much smaller scale, and certainly far more homely, than the Sheats/Goldstein House (see pp 32–5), the Robert and Marjorie Rawlings House demonstrates a range of different concrete techniques from the master of the medium, the American architect, John Lautner. The project sits on Balboa Island enjoying views of Newport Harbour. It is a small house, open and light, which feels much larger than it really is, partly because of the glass wall of the main façade which opens up to create an indoor/outdoor room.

Lautner liked to mix different types and styles of concrete so that the overall effect was not overwhelming. The main wall in the living area in the Rawlings House, for example, has an overlapping finish that makes the wall look like a set of vertical shutters. It is this that provides the decorative focus of the room, while the concrete-domed fireplace – the traditional focal point in a room – is tucked away in a corner. In contrast, when it came to designing the staircase wall, Lautner used a more subtle, horizontal shuttering effect, so that the wall gently recedes into the background without competing with or distracting from the concrete treads of the staircase that cantilever out from it.

Lautner was always particular to acknowledge the work produced by his contractors and craftsmen. In this part of the house, he makes certain that, through his use of a clear plastic balustrade, the skill that has gone into producing this sculptural staircase can be seen and fully appreciated.

At the Rawlings House, Lautner uses light to accentuate the design aspects of his materials. He demonstrates that simply by washing light over the surface of the walls it is possible to reveal the texture of the concrete, thus lifting it into the realm of ornamentation. This is especially apparent in the way that the light filters down from the first floor, highlighting the horizontal pattern left by the formwork on the staircase wall.

Lautner happily uses concrete as both surface decoration and construction material. All his projects were very different from each other – he loathed the rigidity imposed by "styles" and firmly believed that all his houses should reflect their owners' personalities, rather than his own. Hence, concrete, with its flexibility and its ability to lend itself to a multitude of different techniques, enabled him to continue experimenting without ever repeating himself.

↓ LIVING ROOM

A detail of the living room of the Rawlings House showing the domed concrete fireplace tucked neatly into a corner. The pronounced shuttering effect on the walls finds an echo in the stripped wood of the ceiling above.

→ STAIRCASE

Every tread of the staircase can be seen in its entirety, thanks to the see-through perspex balustrade. The staircase demonstrates the skill of the craftsmen employed by Lautner.

HOFFMAN RESIDENCE   ARIZONA 1992 | RICK JOY

Rick Joy, whose practice is based in Tucson, Arizona, USA, has a rather unusual résumé for an architect. For 12 years, before undertaking an architecture degree, he was a musician and carpenter living on the Atlantic coast in the northern state of Maine. After completing his degree in 1990, and following a three-year internship with architect Will Bruder, Joy established his own practice.

In 1993 his hard work paid dividends when he became the recipient of the 'Young Architect of the Year Award' from *Progressive Architecture* magazine. Since then he has won a string of other awards for his innovative ideas. He currently teaches at the Harvard Graduate School of Design.

The Hoffman Residence project involved the remodelling of an original 1957 "case study" type of house, which had been originally designed and built by a contractor who had spent a long time at Frank Lloyd Wright's architectural workshops at Taliesin West, Wisconsin, USA.

The outside of the house consists of a perimeter wall made of concrete, which has been cast *in situ*, as well as more traditional baked adobe, on the inside of which is located a fine, mahogany-framed glass pavilion.

Joy's commission for the current portion of work at the Hoffmann House in Arizona consisted of demolishing the existing garage and reworking the area to create a new master bedroom with adjoining bathroom. Remaining sensitive to the intentions of the original design, Joy's plans incorporate some of the same angles as the existing house. Many of the wall planes are sloped and his palette of materials comprised maple for the walls, ceilings, and cabinets; stainless steel for a feature wall; and concrete, cast in situ, for the fireplace, bathtub, and floors. For the walls and doors, he opted for a combination of frameless sandblasted and clear glass. Inside and on the exterior of the house, Joy juxtaposes different kinds of concrete to great aesthetic effect. In the bathroom, for example, he contrasts the smooth polished floor with the extremely rough-cast bathroom wall, its aggregate clearly visible.

A new garage made from sandblasted concrete block is being built to accommodate the owner's collection of classic Cadillacs dating from the 1930s.

↑ BATHROOM
A view of the bathroom, with its glass-enclosed bath and shower. The rougher concrete wall is part of the original house structure.

← STAIRCASE
Detail of the concrete staircase.

→ FORMER GARAGE
The new master bedroom, formerly the garage, with its smooth, polished, concrete floor. The monolithic concrete fireplace is dissected by the glass wall, so that part of it appears to be outside the house.

SHEEP STATION

AUSTRALIA 1997–8 | DENTON CORKER MARSHALL

Established in 1972, Denton Corker Marshall (DCM) is a major and now long-established Australian architectural practice. Although based primarily in Melbourne and Sydney, the practice has also opened offices throughout Asia and in the UK. They have produced a remarkably diverse body of work, with commissions from the Australian government for embassies in Beijing and Tokyo, the Melbourne Museum, numerous office blocks and hotels, and some spectacular private houses – including this sheep station in the state of Victoria in the southeast of the country.

DCM's work has a strong architectural language, characterized by an interest in spaces and space making – as well as the frames that enclose them. Their work has been described as minimalist, abstract and very conceptual, and concrete is the material that has frequently been used to express their evolving language.

The design of the sheep station has a courtyard as its principal focus. This is almost a gladiatorial arena – dramatic, bare, and with no indication that it is part of a domestic structure.

The plain concrete walls are 4.6 m (15 ft) high and run for almost 200 m (656 ft). Thin in comparison with their height and length, the walls appear as if they are some sort of painted backdrop for a film set, on an overwhelming scale. The house itself is set behind the walls and is reached through a gap in the black concrete section.

This wall is like a huge door surround – larger than the grey wall around it and tilted slightly backward to capture any breezes blowing between the wall and the house behind.

The entrance does not seem particularly inviting at first sight. However, once you have passed through it and into the house, a familiar domestic scale returns. The house has been built as a series of simple, glass-sided boxes offering expansive views over the farm. The floor is polished concrete and continues outside, where it becomes a patio.

The abstract courtyard does have a serious function: in an area of the country where fearsome heat alternates with bitterly cold southwesterly winds blowing up from the sub-antarctic Bass Strait, it acts as a concrete windbreak and sunshade to protect the house, guest house, and sheds behind from the worst of the weather.

The sheep station is a formal architectural essay by DCM, a sculptural experiment exploring the relationship between lines, planes, and voids, with few domestic references. The structural possibilities offered by concrete and its ability to cope with extreme weather conditions have made this design possible. With its severe, massive scale, the house has been endowed with a permanent presence in a wild and hostile landscape. It is a fortress, but a monumental construction with a softer, domestic side.

← ENTRANCE

A detail of the entrance way in the concrete wall that leads to the family living spaces. In the background there is a tantalizing glimpse of the glass-enclosed living room.

→ COURTYARD

A view showing the bleak and virtually bare entrance courtyard, with its contrasting concrete perimeter walls. The black wall tilts back slightly, as if leaning on the shorter wall behind.

CAPE SCHANCK AUSTRALIA 1999 DENTON CORKER MARSHALL

The Cape Schanck project provides another opportunity to look at the work of the pre-eminent Melbourne architectural practice of Denton Corker Marshall (see also pp 48–9). Partner John Denton has summarized their work as being "well mannered, without symbolism or nostalgia". And here is a prime example of the firm's philosophy in practice – there being little in the way of nostalgia to be seen in their approach to the Cape Schanck house.

This is an illustration of the house as object – a black monolith jutting out over a bay in coastal Victoria. Like the Kyneton sheep station in the rural heartland of the state, it is not immediately obvious from the structure of the building that it is a house. Here the traditional domestic iconography has once again been ignored.

The domestic box is clad in sheets of black concrete that at first sight appears to be made of metal. Like the farm house project, the house is in an exposed location, prey to the fickle elements that can change rapidly between blistering heat and wind-driven, lashing rain. Hence, the windows have been placed on the side of the house away from the prevailing wind, situated in a glass ribbon providing views out over the beach. At the end of the box-like structure there is also a massive window that fills the domestic spaces with light.

The client for the house was a designer, who wanted the interior to be simple with a few well-chosen elements. The simple interior echoes the the exterior in form, while the basic concrete floor refers to the exterior construction. The entrance is located underneath the black box. On the main level is the living room, kitchen, and a bedroom, and on the floor below, reached via a con-crete staircase, is a further bedroom and bathroom. The space housing the stairs has a glazed wall that reveals the staircase in section and exposes its structure.

→ EXTERNAL FAÇADE
All clues to the true function of the structure are obscured under sheets of black concrete. The result is a monolithic box with a non-domestic aesthetic typical of the work of Denton Corker Marshall.

← CONTRASTING MATERIALS
In the main living/kitchen area, contrasting
materials, such as the stainless-steel fireplace
and concrete floor, add texture to the room.

SEGAL HOUSE   USA 1979   JOHN LAUTNER

Commissioned by the Segal's, a dance therapist and her husband, architect John Lautner developed a design for a beach-front house that could operate on two levels – both as a home and as a dance studio. Lautner was well known for his close collaboration and working relationship with his clients, an approach that accounts for the fact that his houses are all so very different from each other. Lautner believed listening to be crucial – he listened to his clients' needs and then adapted them to the particular strengths and weaknesses of each individual site, sometimes by maximizing views and spaces here or disguising faults there.

A visitor and architectural student, Henry Whiting, describes his impressions on entering the house: "All the spatial exhilaration is grounded by the concrete wall behind you, which works with the ceiling to feel as though it wraps around you and embraces you. You sense that this is a very comfortable, secure space, yet you are in awe of how dynamic and exciting it can be at the same time." A sentiment that could equally be applied to most of Lautner's other domestic projects.

Whiting goes on to note that: "With Lautner, concrete finds an architect who can create humane, enriching spaces with this often misunderstood material."

Throughout the house shuttered, concrete fireplaces contrast with strip-wood ceilings. The kitchen looks out over the beach, with the curves of the house finding an echo in the curves of the kitchen worktop and the frameless glass window. The ceiling of the living room is a wooden hyperbolic paraboloid. The furniture and furnishings imitate the shapes of boulders, with the organic curves of the house creating a complete, grotto-like environment. The steps, walls, glass, ceiling, and fireplaces all curve in some way, thus creating a series of undulating spaces. It is easy to believe that there is not a single straight line in the entire house. And the amount of foliage and creepers, which have been encouraged to take over the ceilings and walls of the interior rooms and other spaces, heightens the atmosphere of intimate seclusion.

"A cave-like living space curves in from the beach front. This basic concept determined the house, providing a variety of shore and ocean views and creating images that the usual flat-glass front would never allow," is how Lautner described the house.

↓ BEDROOM

The grotto-like bedroom has undulating walls of cast concrete, while the wave-like shuttering on the ceiling reinforces the notion that there are no straight lines anywhere in the house.

→ KITCHEN

In the main kitchen area of the house, the worktop continues to curve out through the room boundary, under the frameless glass wall itself, to form an external window ledge.

GOMEZ-PIMIENTA HOUSE

MEXICO 2000 | TEN ARQUITECTOS

Enrique Norten founded TEN Arquitectos – Taller De Enrique Norten Arquitectos – in 1985 in Mexico City, and Bernardo Gómez-Pimienta joined the practice as a partner in 1987. Then, in 1999, with Barbara Wilks on board as the third partner, the architectural practice of Arch TEN W was founded in New York.

The guiding principle behind the establishment of TEN Arquitectos is: a dedication to creation, and investigation through architecture and design. Over the years, the practice has been involved in projects of many different types of buildings and on many different scales. Furniture design, single-family apartments and houses, commercial and cultural centres, parks, and urban redevelopment projects are just some of the commissions the practice has undertaken. TEN Arquitectos is particularly known for its contemporary approach, using a design vocabulary that "unites the aspirations of the modern world with the traditions of their native Mexican culture and environment" says Gómez-Pimienta.

In 2000, architect Bernardo Gómez-Pimienta decided to build a weekend retreat for himself on the edge of a lake in a small village, just two hours drive from the noise and chaos of Mexico City. The house was constructed on a sloping site with a panoramic view over the lake. A high concrete wall forms the street façade and surrounds the lap pool. This wall also supports a wooden cube set well above the street that holds the water tank.

The house is situated in the historical village of Valle de Bravo, an area where planners try to encourage the use of traditional brick and wood. This is the only concrete house in the village and since nobody locally knew how to build in concrete, every tool had to be brought from Mexico City.

The living space – which also contains the kitchen and dining areas – opens up toward the lake via clear-glass sliding doors. Frosted, sand-blasted glass on the other side of the space screens the patio and pool areas. These glass panels can all be rotated open so that, in effect, the living area is transformed into a completely open platform between the pool/patio and the lake.

The house uses a limited palette of materials. All the walls are made of concrete, the floors and stairs are of travertine marble, while the columns that support the roof are made from stainless steel, as are the handrails throughout the house. The travertine

→ INTEGRATED SPACES
From the pool area, dappled light fills the integrated living and kitchen areas of the house. The travertine marble floor blends harmoniously with the concrete of the kitchen wall.

← BATHROOM
The bathroom lies beyond the kitchen wall
and demonstrates the effective use of a
complementary yet contrasting palette of
glass, stainless steel, concrete and wood.

→ POOL
The poolside floor is made of marble, which
gives more warmth to the space. Above the
concrete wall enclosing the area, the eye comes
to rest on the wood-encased water tank.

marble and the concrete are in design harmony, echoing each other in both tone and pattern.

Gómez-Pimienta has been careful to make sure that the concrete does not dominate the house – instead it is used as a solid feature to contrast with the expanses of glass. Concrete is treated in the same way throughout the house – classic, exposed, cast in situ, raw panels with regular moulding-board screw-holes providing the only decorative motifs.

The kitchen wall, which is more of a solid screen since it isn't full height, hides the main bathroom. Here, the bath has been set into concrete, thus maintaining design continuity between the spaces. The gap between the top of the concrete walls and the roof is filled with glass, giving privacy while maintaining the illusion that

the roof is somehow floating above the structure. Because the materials are neutral in tone, the main colour emphasis comes from the surroundings – the lake, the sky, the clouds, and the vegetation.

The house changes colour throughout the day: yellow, blue, pink, purple, and green depending on the weather. Concrete provides the canvas for this. Gómez-Pimienta explains: "I chose to use concrete because it is a wonderful material – soft, monolithic, and very sensuous. It is at the same time a structural material and a finish and it is apparent how it is made, so there is a handmade aspect to it. A little bit like watercolour, it shows every mistake and allows for no corrections. Concrete is simultaneously very industrial and very handmade; it has the solidity of stone and at the same time the poetry of once having been liquid."

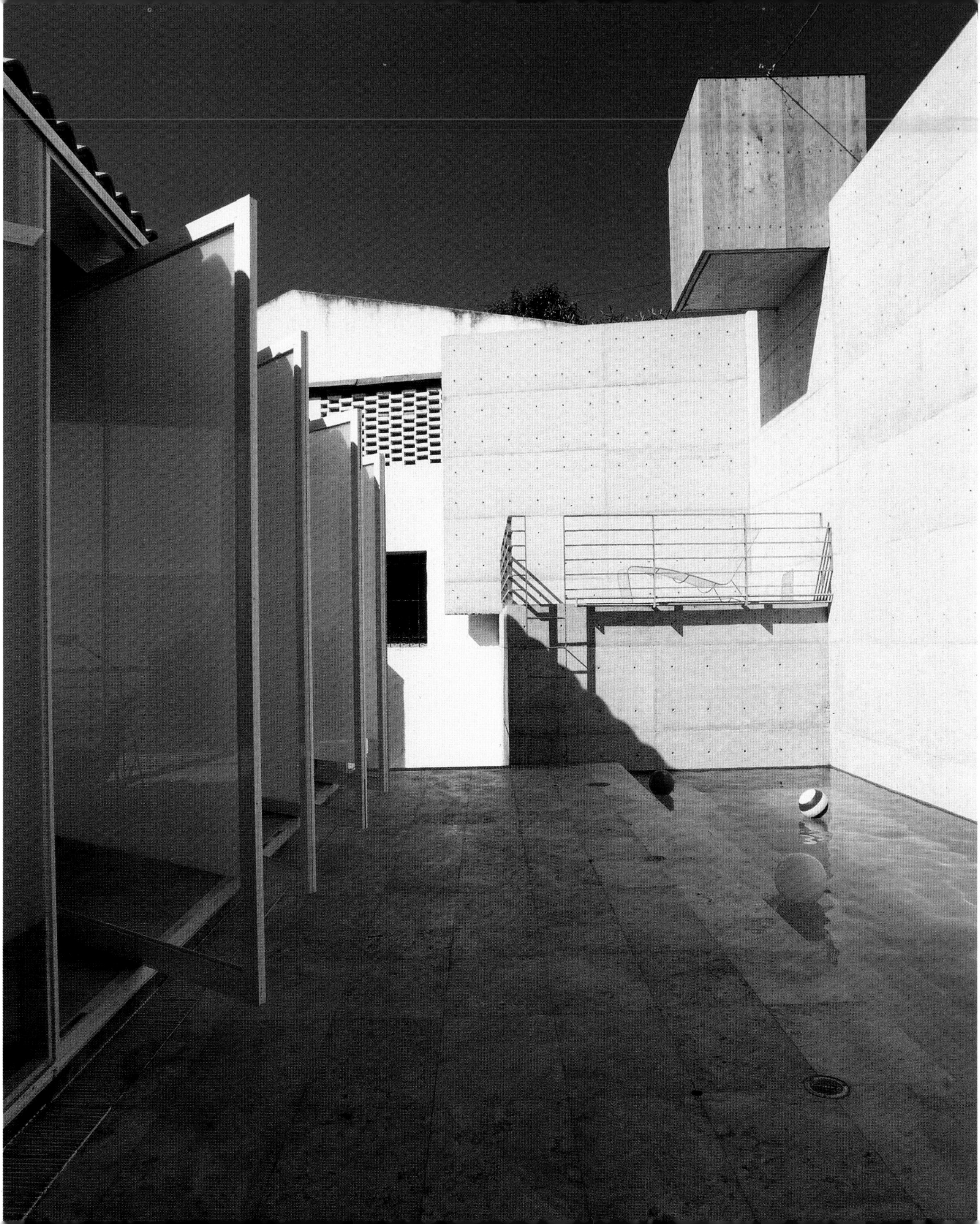

REINER HOUSE   USA 1956–74   JOHN LAUTNER

John Lautner himself best describes the Reiner House in Los Angeles, California, USA: "Two curved walls to the sidelines hide the bedrooms, kitchen, the music room, guest house, and the neighbours' houses. These walls separate the functional areas of the house from the living room and open up the space to the views to both the east and west. The walls were built in brown brick. A low, arched, concrete roof spans over the entire 280 sq m (3,000 sq ft) living area. There are no structural supports to disturb the views and the hilltop is kept practically untouched. The roof was cast in place pre-stressed and post-tensioned in both directions to prevent any cracking." This innovative roof was an experiment in concrete that was to be developed further in Lautner's extraordinary Arango House in Mexico.

"The original client, Kenneth Reiner, wanted to be able to sit at the dining room table and, without moving, but by turning his head, see the ocean to the west, Silverlake to the east, Mount Baldy to the east, and downtown to the southeast" noted Lautner.

Reiner was the perfect client for Lautner. He was a millionaire inventor and manufacturer, who was as keen to experiment as the architect himself, and had the money to do so. He was already a patron of contemporary architecture, having lived in a house by R M Schindler.

Lautner said of the project: "I love this house, it was a pleasure to build and Reiner would not compromise on either materials or design. We travelled abroad to find the perfect finishes. Whatever I wanted was done and the house shows the care that went into it." This care included travelling to look at the work of two of the most important designers of concrete structures in the world – Felix Candela and Pier Luigi Nervi.

The Reiner House project was very significant in the development of Lautner's work, since it was the first time he had created a large, pre-stressed post-tensioned concrete roof. It not only helped to increase the architect's knowledge of the properties of concrete, it also sparked his affinity with the material. Concrete would, henceforth, become Lautner's material of choice. It was also the first project in which Lautner used frameless glass, thanks to the support of his client Reiner, who had prototypes of Lautner's new ideas and gadgets developed in his own factory.

→ LIVING ROOM
A corner of the living room with its architectural concrete fireplace with built-in seat. Pivoting wooden shutters and frameless glass allow undisturbed views of the surrounding countryside.

MÖBIUS HOUSE

| THE NETHERLANDS 1998 | UN STUDIO

The Van Berkel and Bos Architectuur Bureau was founded in Amsterdam, The Netherlands, in 1988 by its principals Ben Van Berkel and Caroline Bos. Together, they have been involved in the design of housing projects, museums, and offices, as well as in the provision of infrastructure planning. In 1998 they established a new firm in addition to Van Berkel and Bos. Called UN Studio, it brought together a network of specialists in architecture, urban development and infrastructure.

The plan for the Möbius House, in Het Gooi, Utrecht, The Netherlands, was based on a Möbius strip – a one-sided mathematical loop twisted to form a continuous surface, and invented by 19th-century German mathematician August Möbius.

The couple who commissioned the house work from home, and so the idea was to create a building containing two offices, built as far away from each other as possible for privacy and space. The other spaces were designed on a loop, where movement would follow the pattern of daily activity. In this way, they would meet in the middle of the house at the end of the day to be together.

As UN Studio says, the house was designed "… as two intertwining paths tracing how two people can live together yet be apart, meeting at certain points, which then become the shared space". The use of concrete made this loop visible, as its structural qualities enabled the architects to make tangible what was in essence a conceptual diagram.

"The structure of movement is transposed to the organization of the two main materials used for the house: glass and concrete. They move in front of each other and switch places. Concrete construction becomes furniture and glass façades turn into interior partitions."

This concept results in some unusual concrete elements throughout the house, such as the dining/living area divider and staircase. Here, concrete is both structural and sculptural. The circular space links the spaces physically but it also reflects the continuity and integration of living and working in the same house. The loop plan is visible as the architecture appears to fold back and over on itself. It is difficult to decide whether you are looking at a concrete house with a glass frame or a glass house framed by concrete elements.

↑ CONCRETE DIVIDER
The concrete divider and staircase in the main dining/living space is structural and sculptural. It also serves as a table top.

→ GLASS AND CONCRETE
In this view of the main living space, the two principal construction materials that have been used – concrete and glass – can be seen, with the concrete staircase visible through the glass.

MAN & WOMAN HOUSE

JAPAN 2000 | NAOYUKI SHIRAKAWA ARCHITECTS

The architect Naoyuki Shirakawa was born in Kitakyushu, Japan, and studied architecture at the University of Kyoto. From 1974 through until 1987 he worked for the practice of Ishimoto Architects before deciding to become independent and set up his own studio, which he did in Tokyo.

Shirakawa's architecture concept is based on geometric forms – the cube, for example, is a shape frequently to be found in his work – and each project has a name. These include the Little House, the Cube House, and the Circular House. In the project illustrated here, known as the Man and Woman House, Shirakawa has taken a simple rectangle and split it down the middle, thus creating identical spaces each side – one for a man and the other for a woman.

As Shirakawa explains: "Compared to European cities, which are normally built with some degree of urban planning, Tokyo is without order and chaotic. The Man and Woman House has a unique structure and makes a unique design statement. There is no traditional division of space for 'kitchen', 'sitting room', and so on inside the building, like in normal houses, but instead it has 'man' and 'woman' divisions. And the house needed some strength in order to make it stand out in a chaotic city like Tokyo – and it was concrete that gave it that strength."

Shirakawa often uses reinforced concrete in the construction of his building projects. In this house, the concrete has been left in its exposed, raw state on the inside as well as the outside. The concrete was poured into old moulds to give it a rougher texture and a warmer finish – something that Shirakawa felt was an entirely appropriate approach for concrete used in a family home. "It may seem contradictory, but concrete is both warm and strong. It has loads of possibilities: being such a flexible material, it could be just about anything," Shirakawa adds.

→ FAÇADE
The house turns away from the street, announcing its presence with a solid concrete façade. The imposing vertical elevation of the house visually combats the chaos of the surrounding city.

→ GLASS
The glass walkway bisecting the building divides the "Man" and "Woman" sides of the house from each other, accentuating the solidity of each enclosure.

→ STAIRCASE

The shoes of the designer occupants of the house line the staircase, denoting the boundaries of the "Man" and "Woman" sides of the house.

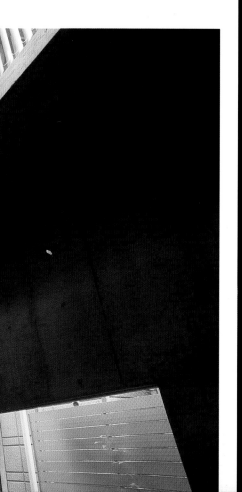

FORM

"The plastic freedom made possible by reinforced concrete." OSCAR NIEMEYER

FORM

Concrete has no natural form, a fact that mightily disturbed the Victorians, who interpreted this as meaning that it was without intrinsic character, that it was an unprincipled, thoroughly pagan material. This accounts partly for the lack of respect given to concrete in the 19th and early 20th centuries. Frank Lloyd Wright himself repeatedly criticized concrete for being without form, stating that it "aesthetically has neither song nor story". But the irony is, that it was this lack of form that gave architects and engineers the ability to create structures and forms previously realized only in their imaginations or sketchbooks. The shell structures of Felix Candela, and the highly sculptural work of Eero Saarinen – take his TWA terminal at JFK Airport, New York, for example – and Oscar Niemeyer.

Though concrete technology is developing all the time, its creative potential is still under-explored, possibly due to a lack of collaboration and dialogue between engineers and architects. As a result, there is a tendency for architects to design with prefab-ricated, precast components that can be assembled like masonry. And while this can often be unsuccessful, there are always exceptions to the rule – Centre Point in central London by Richard Seifert and Partners, was one of the first office towers to make use of precast concrete panels.

Although concrete may be an intrinsically cheap building material, any non-standard component or experimentation can become labour-intensive in an age where labour is scarce and very costly. It isn't surprising, then, that the contemporary examples in this book tend to be houses for seriously wealthy clients or prestigious public projects, such as the Jubilee Line extension for London's underground network or Calatrava's landmark bridge for the Seville Expo in Spain in 1992.

Since then major projects have sprung up that celebrate both the form and surface of the material. Architects such as Oscar Niemeyer have pushed at the technical boundaries of what is possible in concrete construction to create sculptural forms on a scale that was

← FRANK LLOYD WRIGHT
Unity Temple, Oak Park, Illinois, USA (1905–8) by Frank Lloyd Wright. This is Wright's first major concrete slab structure – the slabs are monumental and cantilevering in this imposing religious building. The overhanging portico is shown here. The surface of the concrete is smooth and continuous with sculptural detailing.

→ EERO SAARINEN

The TWA Terminal (now JFK Airport), Idlewild, USA (1956–62) by Eero Saarinen. The qualities of concrete were irresistible to an architect who once wished to be a sculptor.

previously unimaginable. In 1957 Niemeyer was appointed chief architect for the new capital of Brazil, Brasilia. For Niemeyer concrete was the only possible material with the potential to create his vision of Brasilia, with its sensuous, organic forms. He said, "I am not attracted to straight angles or the straight line, hard and inflexible, created by man. I am attracted to free flowing sensual curves."

Peter Collins, in *Concrete: The Vision of a New Architecture*, the only comprehensive history of concrete, published in 1959, notes: "All too frequently concrete merely fulfils the role of a hidden structural support, and derives its aesthetic effects solely from its power to create dramatic forms unseen." When concrete is used to create dramatic forms, he complains, it is still disguised.

Frank Lloyd Wright's approach to the form that concrete should take is entirely different. Not keen on naked concrete, and disapproving of visible joints left from the formwork, Wright thought that concrete should be treated so that its surface appeared smooth and continuous – even recommending lining the formwork with paper to achieve this. Wright exploited the tensile properties of reinforced concrete to create dramatic, sculptural, cantilevering buildings such as Fallingwater, a country retreat for the millionaire Edgar J Kaufmann, at Bear Run in Pennsylvania, USA (1934–7). Cantilevering was, according to Wright, "the most romantic of all structural possibilities."

Early 20th-century concrete enthusiasts felt that the formal possibilities of concrete would result in the creation of a new architectural style. The examples in this chapter demonstrate some contemporary approaches to using the plasticity of the medium on a small scale, creating ranges of sculptural, domestic objects from furniture to lights, or using concrete for something more monumental. All demonstrate the designers' enthusiastic engagement with concrete's plastic possibilities.

← LOUIS KAHN
The Salk Institute, California, USA (1959–65) by Louis Kahn. Kahn studied the components of the Roman Pozzolana in order to achieve a similar colour for his concrete.

→ RICHARD SEIFERT
Centre Point, London, by Richard Seifert and Partners, was one of the first office towers to make use of precast concrete panels.

TABLE, CHAIR, & POT

SWITZERLAND 1952–4, 1999 | WILLY GUHL

Willy Guhl is a little-known designer whose work is, nevertheless, distinctly familiar. His classic Loop chair (originally called the Beach chair) was designed in 1954 for use in the garden. Guhl was born in Stein am Rhein, Switzerland, in 1915, the son of a cabinet-maker. After studying interior architecture at the Kunstgewerbe-schule, Zurich, where he was later to become Professor for Interior Architecture and Industrial Design (1941–80), Guhl set up his own studio in 1939.

Eternit (the name of the manufacturing company and of the glass-fibre, reinforced-concrete material itself) had approached the school in the early 1950s, asking for new ideas as to how their material could be used. Up to that point it had been mainly employed for roofing and wall façades. Most of the academics were appalled by the notion of designing with the material – but not Guhl.

Guhl is interested in all types of material, believing that there are no better or no worse materials, and that each defines its own application and form. The idea of creating solid, rigid forms through the shaping and drying of a pulp fascinated him, and the result has been a 40-year collaboration with Eternit.

Willy Guhl had two of the Loop chairs in his garden and had always wished for a little table to match them. Then, a technical development in the material triggered the design of the Loop table. Eternit fibre cement was initially a conglomeration of cement, min-erals, and asbestos fibre. When asbestos was banned, this component was replaced by cellulous fibre, which resulted in a bulkier product. He modified the design of the chair to cope with the new material and developed the table at the same time.

Guhl has also designed a range of flowerpots for Eternit that have sold literally in their millions over the years. His products are sold through Wohnbedarf, a company set up in 1931 as one of the first retailers, manufacturers, and distributors of the light and func-tional modern furniture as espoused by the Bauhaus.

Although today it is common to find his Loop chairs used indoors, Guhl makes it clear that the chair was, in every respect, designed for outdoor use. "People send me pictures of their chairs, they paint flowers on them, they upholster them; its their chair, let them do with it as they want. But I still would not put one in my living room."

← SPINDLE POT
Guhl designed the Spindle pot in 1952, in collaboration with his students. This large-scale planter has become a design classic.

↓ LOOP TABLE
The Loop table was designed in 1999 – more than 40 years after the Loop chair. The table contains two circular apertures to accommodate glasses.

→ LOOP CHAIR
A view of Guhl's sculptural Loop chair, which he designed in 1954. Modifications in the design were necessary due to the change from asbestos to cellulose fibre used in its construction.

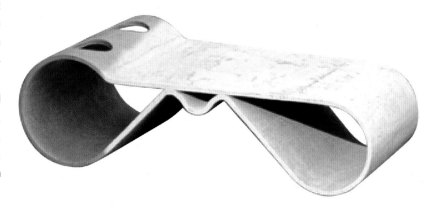

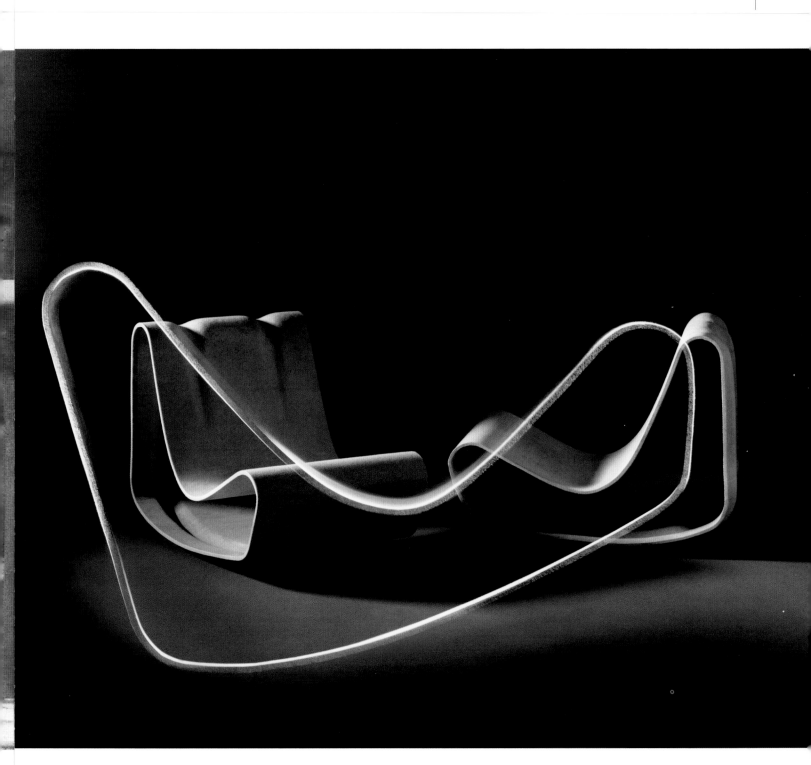

CURVY WORK UNIT UK 1999 TOTEM DESIGN

Totem (Ian Hume and Catherine Phillips) has established an enviable reputation as architectural designers of concrete in both the domestic and commercial interior. They have been constantly working toward perfecting a uniform and continuous work surface made out of concrete.

In this domestic kitchen project, the designers have emphasized both the chunkiness and plasticity of concrete by creating an undulating worktop that looks as though it has been shaped by a jigsaw, echoing the shape of the MDF (medium-density fibreboard) shelves beneath. The combination of utilitarian MDF and concrete in the same unit is a nice touch, since both materials form the backbone of contemporary construction, yet both are usually covered over or disguised in some way in order to hide their nature and character. Hume describes this approach as "a play on honest materials."

Hume is keen on the design from the 1960s and 70s – in fact, he lives and works in a 1960s interior created by his parents – and these design influences can readily be seen in the curvaceous worktop. Totem is currently working on a larger-scale interior project, consisting of a staircase, worktop, and cantilevering fireplace, all made out of concrete. The company has also perfected a new type of sealant that makes the concrete surface totally impervious to any abrasive material or acid-containing agents. This represents a major advance, making concrete even more suitable for use as kitchen worktops. As Hume says: "We used to tell people to take care of their worktops but of course they rarely did; this new sealant means that they don't have to. We now feel confident we have solved a major problem area." Totem is also investigating the possibility of designing and producing its own range of sinks and basins made from concrete, and it is constantly being asked to produce baths as well.

Hume is keen to produce baths, but the problem to be overcome here is the development of heating elements that can be inserted within the concrete. Since the concrete absorbs heat, the bath water goes cold very quickly if the bath itself is not heated. Totem believes the material still has lots of potential to be explored and is now transferring some of the techniques and knowledge it has developed while working with concrete to another rather neglected material – plastic.

↑ → WORKSTATION

The organic shape of the workstation doubles as a food-preparation area and a breakfast bar. Despite its weight, the concrete-formed worktop seems to float above the MDF shelves that replicate its curvaceous form.

KITCHEN & BATHROOM   UK 2001   KAYODE LIPEDE

Kayode Lipede's interest in concrete was first sparked while he was still an architecture student at the Architectural Association in London, though at the time he was more inspired by the improbability of concrete boats than concrete buildings. In 1996, after completing his studies, he set up his own company designing and manufacturing concrete furniture and fittings for houses and bars. Lipede likes to use concrete as structurally as possible, creating walls, floors, and major objects such as baths and worktops, so that he can utilize the qualities of the material to the fullest extent.

Lipede is hands-on by instinct, and through experimentation has developed his own mixes and his own concrete recipes. The nuances of shade he can achieve through his mastery of the mix means that he can now produce more than 50 distinct shades of grey, ranging from duck grey to grey-white. Lipede does not like to add pigments, preferring instead to introduce colours by changing the types of sand. "I like natural tones and would rather not use pigments at all." He is also particular about the types of aggregate used, believing that jagged stones are more suitable to terrazzo. For concrete he prefers the effect produced by rounder aggregates, such as pea shingle, which he believes are part of the "signature of concrete".

Lipede's repertoire of concrete creations is growing all the time, and now he has produced worktops, floors, baths, benches, and fireplaces, and he is currently exploring the possibilities of producing concrete plank walls. More than 90 per cent of his work is now made on site, creating objects in their own environment.

"The material becomes what you make it," Lipede explains. "Concrete offers you a clean slate." The advantages gained from its use in domestic interiors are varied, as concrete can be repolished and resealed again and again – tired worktops and floors can be made to look brand new once more. And because concrete is porous, the material really absorbs the sealant, making it quite an impermeable surface. It can also be made to any precise thickness you like, an advantage it has over stone.

Lipede feels that concrete is at its best when used with weight. Its heaviness and thickness can initially seem daunting to clients, but the possibility of creating chunky elements is part of its character and he finds clients respond to this once they see the final results.

In addition, as Lipede explains: "One of the advantages of working with concrete is that you don't have to have seams and joints, as you would if using, say, marble or granite – it also means that you can produce work that is more sculptural in concept."

With his expertise, passion, and continuing experimentation, Lipede will certainly be developing new ways of introducing concrete into the home in the future.

↓ CONCRETE & STEEL

A stainless-steel sink and single tap unit inserted directly into the white concrete sinktop, which incorporates an integral drainer, add interest and contrast.

→ INTERIOR AND COURTYARD

Interior and courtyard, South Kensington, London by Ziggurat. The wavy, in situ concrete bench in the courtyard is by Ziggurat and Lipede.

STOOL & PLANT HOLDER

Rachel Reynolds founded The Shed in 1999 after spending a year experimenting and producing prototypes of concrete furniture. Reynolds initially studied metal design at college, producing everything from cutlery to sculpture, and after graduating worked for the designer Ron Arad before setting up on her own. Since establishing a metal workshop would have been enormously expensive, Reynolds decided to work in concrete instead. She literally set up business in her shed, and with little power or equipment available she had to produce everything by hand in basic concrete.

Now the process has become more complicated, incorporating lots of resins and latex to make the concrete less brittle. Reynolds also experiments with lightweight aggregates, such as Pearlite, to help reduce the weight of some of the heavier stools and benches. More recently, she has worked with Bylite – polystyrene beads covered with cement paste – to form a lightweight aggregate.

Because her stools were originally intended for garden use, their design is very organic, to fit better with the natural landscape. It is unusual for concrete to be used to create organic forms, though, of course, its plasticity and the fact that it has no form of its own make it an eminently suitable material. No doubt this aesthetic is due to Reynolds' sculpture training. Now that the stools are creeping inside the home, however, she has developed coffee tables, fireplaces, and pots to complement them. Once concrete furniture moves into the domestic interior, Reynolds believes: "It should be used sparingly, as a feature for effect, rather than *en masse.*"

The stools have an impasto-like finish, partly because they are made by trowelling concrete onto a wire frame so that the trowel strokes are obvious. Reynolds' pots look even rougher. The concrete is a dryish mix – which means it cracks and crumbles more and the aggregate stays on the surface – and it is poured into moulds lined with scrunched-up polythene, which leaves a textured imprint on the pot. Reynolds highlights these "wrinkles" by filling them with cement of a different shade. After which "I hit it with a hammer," she says, "to knock off excess lumps. It is also very therapeutic."

← STOOLS

Reynolds works with basic concrete pigments of white, grey, and black, also occasionally adding earth colours but eschewing brighter colours. These, she feels, are not only liable to fade, they are also inappropriate. This is very much in line with her belief that, "why use concrete if you are going to make it look like something else?".

← ↓ PLANT HOLDERS
The rough-textured finish on these plant holders was achieved by lining the moulds with scrunched-up polythene before pouring the concrete mix in on top of it.

OXO LIGHT | UK 1999 | PETER WYLLY

The stylish concrete Oxo light was designed by Peter Wylly for his company, Babylon. Wylly was born in Leicester, England, in 1967 and went on to study fashion design. Despite his fashion design background, when he established his own business in 1991, at the age of just 24, it was to take advantage of a new production technique he had invented for making lamp shades. In 1997 he formed Babylon designs with Birgit Israel, designing and producing lighting and accessories, as well as creating special products for well-known high-street outlets such as Habitat, Conran, The Body Shop, and Ambiente.

In 1999 Wylly launched Babylon London – a collection of lighting and accessories, including designs by Michael Anastassiades, Torsten Neeland, and Matthew Hilton. Wylly is now diversifying his business interests and is launching an e-mail messaging system and planning to open a Babylon-designed and co-owned hotel in Provence, France, in 2002, which will feature many new Babylon-designed products.

The Oxo light was designed to work like a building block, so that individual lighting units could be stacked together in any configuration desired by the user. As this type of usage was part of the initial design concept, it was important to use a material that did not have an "ugly" side. In this way, the light had neither a front nor a back.

Talking of the early development of his light, Wylly explains: "We first produced Oxo in plaster, but after prolonged usage – 48 hours, non-stop – the heat was such that the plaster would pop and split into two pieces. Luckily, concrete doesn't do this." But Wylly's use of concrete was not merely pragmatic; aesthetically, he likes "the honesty of concrete, it is self-coloured, self-textured, and self-finished".

Wylly also enjoys working with other materials, including ceramic and wood. One problem he feels with concrete is that it is still perceived as being a cheap material. But the production costs – especially when working on a small scale – are high, and customers don't understand why pieces can be so expensive.

In his own loft home in Shoreditch, East London, Wylly has installed heating under the concrete floor. "This is the best type of heating you can get. In the winter what you would normally think of as being a cold floor becomes a huge, low-temperature radiator. We can walk around barefoot all winter – a real luxury."

→ STACKING LIGHTS

The Oxo lights work well when stacked together to create sculptural elements. Because they have no back or front they can be assembled in any number of different ways.

SINK

UK 2000 | ADAM BLACKBURN

While studying at college, Adam Blackburn supplemented his day-to-day living by working on construction sites. It was here, as he watched concrete being used in the building trade, that he realized there were possibilities for the application of concrete in more interesting, and certainly more creative ways. As his work at college progressed, Blackburn found himself increasingly intrigued by the design possibilities of concrete, not just because of the range of textures offered by this material, but also because of its "potential for three-dimensional moulding".

Blackburn's sink on legs was an early attempt to explore the inherent design potential of cast concrete. He built the formwork incorporating the profiles that resulted in the drainer channels, demonstrating concrete's adaptability when it comes to producing crisp detailing.

The main drawback to making objects from ordinary concrete is the dead weight of the finished artefacts. In this regard, Blackburn was impressed with the chunkiness he achieved but he is now looking at a variety of different techniques for lightening the load. As other designers working in this field have discovered, adding lightweight aggregates to the concrete mix offers definite possibilities.

Blackburn has also experimented with combining concrete with other materials. His sink, for example, rests on strong, stainless-steel legs. The sink is intended to be freestanding, rather than inserted into a worktop where, apart from the interior and outer rim, it would largely be hidden. When seen exposed like this, it "reveals its true shape and monolithicness" – it also gives it a truly sculptural presence. Blackburn's work is now leading him in a different direction: trying more unusual aggregates, such as iron filings. Once the concrete has set, he grinds back the surface to reveal the metal and then polishes it to create a striking contrast.

Inevitably, the design of his sink is resulting in commissions for baths and other monolithic pieces. However, concrete and water may not seem like a natural combination – after all, some people's preconceptions about concrete stem from seeing the ugly water-stained, exterior concrete walls towering above them. This occurs largely as a result of inadequate drainage combined with poor maintenance. But today, the resins, additives, and sealants that are readily available mean that this is less likely to occur. With the concrete impermeable to water, the surfaces of sinks, baths, and showers remain unstained.

← ↓ SINK AND DRAINER

The extreme chunkiness of this cast-concrete sink, an early Blackburn project, suggests that the bowl and draining board have both been carved out of a single block.

RINGS & BOWLS   UK 2000   KELVIN BIRK

Attracted by the plasticity of concrete, gold and silversmith Kelvin Birk has been experimenting by teaming one of the cheapest building materials with a range of precious metals and stones.

In Birk's rings and pendants, concrete is sandwiched between smooth silver, while in other examples, precious stones, such as diamonds, are embedded in it – thus creating the most expensive of aggregates. Kelvin likes the idea of the diamond being found in the concrete that surrounds it, as it is "like finding a precious stone in a mountain". In other experiments he has introduced paint pigments into the mix to produce coloured rings and earrings that look more like a semi-precious stone than concrete.

Some of Birk's other experiments have involved casting concrete bowls from plaster moulds for a smooth finish. These are then gilded inside the rim to transform cheap, utilitarian objects into something altogether more luxurious. He has tried many types of mix, sometimes taking the bowl out of the mould before it has fully set, to impart a rougher finish. Ironically, he found it harder to produce a rough surface than a smooth one, but by adding more sand to the mix, the results are rougher and more textured. He has also found that drier mixes give a rougher finish. There is still a craft quality to working with concrete on this scale. Birk discovered, for example, that if, when making his rings and earrings, the concrete dried too quickly it would simply crumble. To overcome this, he had to inhibit the drying process, stretching it over an entire day.

Although many people have found Birk's fascination with concrete strange, for him the attraction lies in the unpredictable nature of the results: "concrete is controllable up to a point but you still are never quite sure how it will look when it comes out of the mould. And that is part of its attraction, all the pieces are unique."

↓ SANDWICH RING
A thin layer of concrete, with its aggregate clearly visible, has been sandwiched between two thin slivers of silver to make this ring.

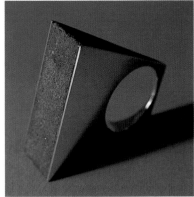

← ↑ WEDGE RING
Here, the concrete surface of the ring is far more prominent, more wedge-like, and a finer aggregate has been used to make the concrete core.

↑ → BOWLS

Two different versions of Birk's bowls can be
seen here. In the example above, a silver liner
has been added to produce a luxurious finish;
in the other, right, a more utilitarian finish has
been achieved by leaving the concrete unlined.

LOFT APARTMENT

Designed by architects Buschow Henley, the concrete dividing walls in this loft apartment act as the major defining sculptural elements of the design. The two concrete dividers or, as architect Simon Henley describes them, "emblematic maquettes", are constructed from pre-cast concrete planks 1500 x 100 x 150 mm (5 ft x 4 x 6 in). At one end, alternate planks are absent, allowing the adjacent planks to cantilever. Part of a band near the top of one of the dividers is wooden rather than concrete, and this simple transition helps to relieve the huge mass and create a relationship with the wooden bathroom doors behind. It also acts as a reference to the imprint left in the concrete from the timber formwork used in the casting process. The result is a wall that appears light, almost delicate.

Buschow Henley had originally wanted to cast in situ, but soon realized that casting a wall on the second floor was not a practical proposition. The recessed lighting installed both above and below the dividers casts a warm glow over the surface. The way the concrete is illuminated makes a significant difference to our perception of it – here, for example, it seems warm and comforting.

Henley is slightly tongue in cheek in his design approach to concrete. By using it in a highly simplified, very mannered way, he exploits the material for its sculptural and decorative qualities, rather than its constructional ones. The new concrete has a resonance seen against the original concrete used in the building's shell, and the whole project is, for Henley, an exercise in construction. His client, who admires the work of the artist Richard Serra, had asked for a concrete monolith – an idea that appealed to the architect. Even in a domestic interior, Henley believes it is unnatural, a denial of the qualities of the material, to make small things out of concrete.

The concrete has a waterproof additive, a necessary precaution as the back of one wall acts as the splashback to the shower, with its concrete shower tray. Because of the timber formwork, the perfect, flush line of the concrete planks in the living space side has resulted in some unevenness on the shower side, which has taken on a rather attractive, weatherboard effect. Simon Henley is the first to admit that concrete construction techniques are not yet perfect, despite architects' best efforts. He does not like what he calls "boutique finishes" and "concrete tokenism", and his aim is to apply his concrete plank construction on a grander scale.

↑ UNIFIED CONCEPT

The concrete planks making up the dividers have been laid in a stretcher band pattern, in the same manner as the original brick walls and new ply floor, so mimicking and uniting the different elements and materials.

↓ → DIVIDERS

In these views, it can be seen how the parallel concrete walls have been arranged to screen the storage and bathroom areas from the main, open space of the loft area.

FIREPLACES   UK 2000   CVO FIRE

Carolyn and Christian van Outersterp established CVO Fire in 1999, after Carolyn had been working for a traditional fireplace manufacturer. Their aim has been to re-establish the fireplace as the focus of the domestic living room and to create an awareness of its contemporary design possibilities. Bringing their previous experience – she as a fashion designer, he as a landscape architect – to bear, the van Outersterps have produced a range of designs in concrete that embody both the function and the aesthetics of fire.

Responding to current interior design trends, CVO's fireplaces and hearths are made of glass-fibre reinforced concrete in pale, off-white shades. They are hand-finished to create a smooth, almost stone-like effect. Only one fireplace in their range is coloured, the concrete pigmented to produce a jade green surround.

Using glass fibre allows CVO to cast its concrete creations as thinly as possible, and it also means that complex shapes not possible with any other material can be produced. Even so, the fireplaces are heavy – the Ripple weighs in at a hefty 275 kg (600 lb). The concrete is sealed, but to preserve its natural appearance it is not given a varnished finish. The surface is then hand-finished, literally scrubbed to remove any surface imperfections.

CVO uses a range of aggregates, so some fireplaces appear more textured than others. And due to the malleability of the concrete, other materials, such as bronze and lead crystal, can easily be incorporated into the designs – often to stunning effect.

The company also produces fire bowls – cast oval or circular designs in either black or white concrete. These freestanding bowls act as the grate for many of the fireplaces. They can be used with solid fuel or, if teamed with Ceramat, with a gas fire, too. This material was first manufactured by the American aerospace industry to prevent the space shuttle from breaking up during re-entry into the Earth's atmosphere. It produces a ripple of fire that appears almost to float on the bowl. An advantage the concrete bowl has over metal is that it never becomes as hot, and so is safer.

CVO is continually experimenting and plans to expand its range to include concrete hearth benches and other elements. As Carolyn van Outersterp says: "We use concrete because of its fluidity and flexibility. We use it to create sculptural elements that are durable, heat-resistant and with the visual and textural qualities of stone."

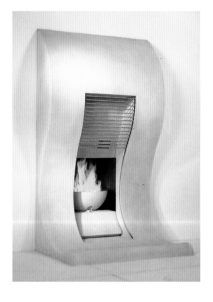

↑ RIPPLE FIRE
This concrete surround holds a convex iron guard that can be lowered over the fire.

↑ SLIT AND SLAB FIRE
The fireplace that imitates a piece of abstract art.

→ GEOMETRIC PLANE
This fireplace has become a major architectural element incorporating seating and, if required, storage for logs.

↓ FIRE BOWLS (below left and right)
Fire bowls, produced in black or white concrete, with detachable concrete grates.

SAG TABLE THE NETHERLANDS 2000 | JESSE VISSER

When you first see this table, with its wafer-thin, curving top, it is difficult to believe that it is, in fact, made out of concrete. It defies all the stereotypes that define concrete objects which state that they should be heavy and rectilinear. Jesse Visser designed the Sag Table for his graduation show in the three-dimensional design department of the Utrecht Arts School in The Netherlands. The table has won a number of design prizes and was part of Droog Design's collection shown at the Milan Furniture Fair in 2000.

The Sag Table does indeed dip in the middle – being 5 cm (2 in) lower in the centre than it is at the edges. Explaining his thinking behind the table's unique design, Visser believes that "the energy and concentration is directed to the lowest point, where the user sits". The dimensions of the table are 200 x 100 x 75 cm (approximately 78 x 39 x 29 in). In section, the table forms part of a circle that would have a diameter of 50 m (164 ft). "When one sits in the middle of the table, the tabletop curves up from the sitter and so the items on the table do not stand completely vertically, making one think about the relationship between product and consumer," says Visser. Concrete, the designer believes, "stimulates one's tactile senses, but seems completely adept at keeping its original form."

With concrete used in this fashion, strength is an important consideration, and so the tabletop is made out of reinforced concrete that is 2 cm (¾ in) thick. The structure of the tabletop is very compact and strong because as little water as possible has been added to the concrete mix. It is reinforced with two layers of fibreglass to form the strong, rigid surface that is required for safety. After the concrete has been poured, the mould is covered with a thin sheet of polystyrene to produce the very smooth surface of the finished table.

→ TABLE
As the name suggests, the top of the Sag table dips in the middle, giving the impression of a slender, flexible top, in contrast with the rigid solidity of the legs.

THE STONES | USA 1998 | MAYA LIN

The artist and designer Maya Lin is best known for her Vietnam Veterans' Memorial in Washington DC, designed in 1981 – a commission she won in competition while still an undergraduate at Yale University. Trained as both an artist and architect, her work reflects her response and sensitivity to nature, specifically the unique conditions of landscape and topology; her interest in the shifting boundary of the horizon; and her use of natural materials.

In her sculpture, this inspiration from nature is often combined with Eastern aesthetics, resulting in work displaying a dignified restraint and subtlety. As Lin herself says: "I am inspired by landscape, topography, and natural phenomena, but it's the landscape from a 20th-century perspective; landscape through the lens of technology. It's how we see the world, how our view has been shaped by new technologies. It's a satellite image of the Earth, a microscopic image of cells." Given this approach, the use of concrete as a contemporary technique seems entirely appropriate for Lin's execution of some of these ideas.

In 1998 Lin designed the Stones collection – part of a larger collection for Knoll International, entitled The Earth is (not) Flat. Her contribution includes low, elliptical, concrete tables with slightly convex tops and two sizes of elliptical stools with slightly concave seats. Designed for use indoors and out, the Stones are constructed of hollow, lightweight, fibreglass-reinforced concrete – thus combining the strength and lightness of fibreglass with the durability and longevity of concrete. Their unexpected lack of weight combined with their sculptural qualities mean that the Stones fall somewhere between art and design. The Stones collection reflects Lin's love of the land, and their elliptical shapes and subtle curves have echoes in much of the artist's work.

The Stones were the first pieces that Maya Lin designed for Knoll International. "I realized that the furniture with which we are all familiar is derived primarily from a Western European tradition. My husband collects pre-Columbian art, and he has several stone *metate*, or ancient thrones, which have slightly concave tops; he also has some porcelain pillows from China. These non-Western objects struck me as profoundly beautiful and became the inspiration for my designs. The forms are cast in reinforced concrete, which creates a soft, smooth surface, like those of the ancient stone chairs."

→ STOOLS

The Stones stools and tables can be used with the same dramatic effect inside or out. Coloured pigments in five earth colours have been added to the concrete – slate grey, grey-blue, pale green, pale yellow, and terracotta – as a reference to Maya Lin's concern for nature and the planet.

TEXTURE

Concrete is always cast in some way, either by being poured into a mould or, on a more industrial scale, into formwork. In general, moulds produce a smooth finish, while formwork leaves behind an impression of whatever material has been chosen for the shuttering. Another factor important in determining surface texture is the size, quantity, and types of aggregate used in the mix.

Texture implies an overall surface pattern, such as the characteristic timber grain from rough wood shuttering. But texture can also be produced by working on the surface mortar to reveal the aggregate beneath. In the 1960s and 70s it was not unusual to see the best architects and designers taking an innovative approach to the public face of concrete, sometimes blasting patches of it away or tooling the surface with a drill. Alas, the price of labour today makes this approach impossibly expensive.

Formwork concrete produces a variety of surface textures and patterned effects simply by casting concrete against roughly sawn wooden boards. What was simply a utilitarian, inexpensive finish developed into something more when architects started to specify certain woods and carefully positioned boards to reflect part of their design. Companies now make standard plastic moulds that reproduce the imprint of wood, proof indeed of the popularity of the effect – even if it is a deceit. Architect Tadao Ando uses skilled carpenters to create the moulds for his concrete to ensure the quality of the finished material. "The high standard of Japanese concrete building is based on our woodworking heritage. Concrete moulds must be made with great care and precision to produce a clean and perfect surface. As a matter of fact, I used to employ joiners to make my moulds."

Frank Lloyd Wright explored texture in a typically innovative way, experimenting with the decoration through modular concrete blocks cast from profiled moulds. "The idea was to combine metal reinforcement with precast blocks running a textile-like warp and weft of metal rods in hollowed joints between the blocks and then filling the hollows with protecting cement." Taking this a stage further, Wright designed perforated decorative blocks, as seen in the Pfieffer Chapel, where the design harks back to intricate medieval wooden rood screens.

The modernist movement didn't hold with surface decoration, however, and although admired for its structural possibilities,

← THE NATIONAL THEATRE
The National Theatre, London, UK (1967–70) by Denys Lasdun. The theatre foyer with the clear imprint of the wooden formwork creating a boldly textured concrete rarely seen in interiors today.

→ STORER HOUSE
John Storer House, Los Angeles, California, USA, by Frank Lloyd Wright. In this interior Wright uses modular concrete blocks to create sculptural, decorative walls.

concrete was rarely explored in terms of texture in the pre-war years. The marks left behind by formwork and other marks of construction later became acceptable as they were seen to be part of the nature of the material and, therefore, true to it, but in pre-war Modernist buildings it was common practice to whitewash or even render the concrete to cover these "flaws".

Inspired by American industrial buildings – the giant, monolithic silos of the grain belt, for example, and the huge granary elevators – the roughness of cheap, utilitarian construction was seen, post-war, very much as a plus. As Le Corbusier wrote: "Let us listen to the counsels of American engineers, but let us beware of American architects", Wright included.

In those post-war years, in the Unité d'Habitation, Tourdet, and The Chapel at Ronchamp, Le Corbusier explored the design potential of pattern and texture in concrete – both rough formwork and carefully moulded patterns. Texture was also an important part of architecture in the 1960s and 70s, when monumental tooling and highly intricate and abstract moulded friezes and sculptured panels proliferated. Compare those buildings with the work of today, in the proliferaton of smooth-finished, fair-faced concrete typified by the much-imitated work of Tadao Ando.

A growing interest in the work of Denys Lasdun, Allison and Peter Smithson, John Lautner, and Richard Seifert, among others, and an appreciation of projects that were once derided, such as the South Bank in London, with its wonderful examples of formwork textures, mean that a generation of young architects are beginning to explore and adapt their techniques, hopefully bringing texture back into the contemporary concrete vocabulary.

The examples of the designers' and architects' work provided in this chapter demonstrate just some of the uses of textured concrete – both rough and smooth – in the domestic environment. They illustrate the subtlety and precision of this material and, hopefully, open up a new range of possibilities.

↑ CAROLE VINCENT
Artist Carole Vincent uses pigments to colour her dramatic, vibrant concrete sculptures.

→ JOHN OUTRAM
A detail of John Outram's Adenbrooks Hospital, Cambridge, UK, showing his colourful, textured "Blitzcrete"; a concrete developed by the architect.

STREET-PORTER HOUSE | UK 1992 | PIERS GOUGH

Piers Gough studied at the Architectural Association in London before setting up Campbell, Zogolovitch, Wilkinson and Gough in 1975. CZWG are renowned for their housing projects, offices, new galleries for the National Portrait Gallery, and an award-winning public toilet in Notting Hill, London. In this commission for a house in the Clerkenwell area of London, for the media personality Janet Street-Porter, concrete has been used in a variety of ways.

The traditional concrete construction has been left exposed, hinting not only at a trend seen in many local loft apartments, but also in response to his client's wishes that her new home should "look a bit wrecked".

Throughout the house, the precast concrete ceiling beams have standard concrete posts inserted between them. In the bedroom, the ceiling contrasts with the more sophisticated polished maple-wood floor, though the industrial aesthetic is carried through to the bed –

an aluminium trolley from an industrial supplier. On the concrete screed floors, yellow pigment gives a sandy look, while elsewhere shards of marble appear to have been tossed into the still wet mix.

Gough is known as a colourist and believes that in a domestic interior, "You can have too much grey. I wanted to add terracotta, plaster and give colour to the concrete to warm it up." On the ground floor the colours are dark ochres, but these become progressively lighter as you move up through the house. This effect is mirrored on the exterior, where the brick is in four shades, from dark brown at the bottom to cream at the top.

Gough has explored the potential of concrete in this project, in both precast form and that poured *in situ*, using the material in a lively, colourful, curvaceous, and warm way. The result is a distinctive, individual, and light-hearted contrast to its more commonly austere use in contemporary interiors.

→ STAIRCASE

The staircase of the London home of journalist
and television personality Janet Street-Porter is
also made of concrete, with a concrete render
dado spreading organically from the stair treads
up the wall, as if growing on the surface like
some sort of lichen.

← BEDROOM

The client wanted an effect that suggested the
building had aged, using raw concrete in a way
that implied that the material was already worn
and old – a look that the material would take on
if it had been gradually exposed over time.

BATH   USA 2000   TYLER HAYS

Tyler Hays is an artist whose appreciation for space and obsession with materials led him in 1994 to found, along with architects Scott Glass and Joshua Vogel, the multi-disciplinary design company BDDW. Since that time, Hays' work has ranged in scope and scale from designing buildings to designing products and furniture for Manhattan boutiques, while simultaneously exhibiting his own artwork. The company has also opened a shop in New York displaying a range of furniture, furnishings, BDDW's palette of materials, and product prototypes.

Hays designs from the inside out. Nowhere is this more apparent than in his own home, which he treats as an artwork in form and function. Constantly evolving and a perpetual work in progress, Hays sees his living space as a blank canvas. He often focuses on a single piece, surrounding that initial object with both similar and complementary works. He began designing his home, located in the industrial area of Williamsburg, Brooklyn, USA, around a conceptual cast-concrete bathtub. Loosely based on the Japanese art of bathing, the concrete tub is washed in warm daylight from a skylight placed directly above it. Hays chose concrete in order to emphasize the tub's architectural weight and mass. He recognized a certain freedom in the properties of the material, afforded by its simplicity and economic viability. "What I really love about the bathtub in this space is how it never really tells us if it is brutal, exposed, and severe in its placement and material, or whether it is richly warm, lush, and romantic. Using concrete's humility lets you see past the materiality, at its function, giving the material in turn its own beauty." It was only after the bath had been constructed that Hays began mixing materials such as mahogany, plywood, and walnut, with a collection of found objects to create the interior space.

Hays believes that the material really just responds to the way designers use it. "Concrete stands alone. It is a cheap liquid that you simply pour and form into structural stone. Its beauty certainly lies deeper than its surface, which is really the material as function. The semantics behind how concrete is used has dramatically furthered and regressed architecture and design. It would be nice to blame or give credit to this simple material, but it commands a certain self-evaluation. The freedom it affords makes an architect closer to 100 per cent responsible for the outcome."

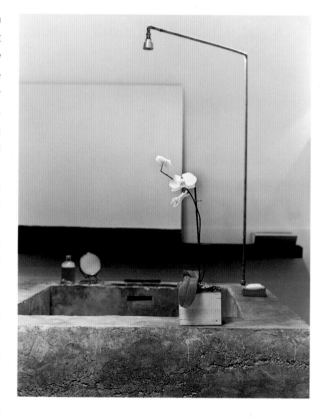

↑ → BATH

The blockish form of the concrete bath becomes the principal focal point in the bathroom space, its roughly textured surface needing little in the way of additional ornamentation.

PLANTERS | UK 2000 | KATHY DALWOOD

Kathy Dalwood's work displays the influence of two of her passions: post-war architecture and sculpture. Her father was the well known sculptor Hubert Dalwood, who explored landscape and the intervention of man in nature through his abstract work.

"All his work was produced through casting, and as children we spent lots of time in his studio watching, 'helping', and making our own small casts in plaster, and I'm sure this had an influence on my interest in these processes," says Kathy Dalwood.

Not wanting to study sculpture for fear of following in her father's footsteps, Dalwood studied and then taught fine art, as well as designing one-off furniture throughout the 1980s, later moving into batch production with her Cast collection of concrete planters.

The design references for these pieces come from modernist architecture and civil engineering, including bridges, silos and water towers. As Dalwood notes," I was drawn by the economy and asymmetry of these monolithic structures and was intrigued by the idea of reducing their scale and yet making work that still retains a strong three-dimensional feel. The process of casting is a fascinating one. The evidence of fabrication and casting is so visible in concrete structures: mould lines, changes in tone, and imperfections actually help to define their intrinsic qualities. Working with moulds is exciting because initially you have to construct something that doesn't really exist — the negative of the intended positive. Taking the cast from the mould is an intense but compulsive moment. When I look at buildings or bridges constructed from cast concrete, I'm fascinated to think of engineers using the same process, but on a gigantic scale." Dalwood not only explores the form and traces left by casting in her pieces but also, unusually for small-scale concrete work, the use of exposed aggregates.

"I was intrigued by the raw textures of the aggregates when seen close up. I thought it would be interesting to make elegant, domestic pieces from this somewhat brutal material, which usually has large-scale, industrial applications." It is also a finish used for external decoration, and so its move into the interior — and the domestic interior at that — is doubly unusual and disconcerting. Using aggregate innovatively in this fashion challenges our perceptions and prejudices of the "Brutalist" buildings where this technique is commonly found and which Dalwood so obviously admires.

← ↓ DOMESTIC PLANTERS

The rough and the smooth — two types of concrete used by Dalwood to create her domestic planters. The smooth type displays the impression of the mould that was used to make them, while the exposed-aggregate type provides a texture of its own.

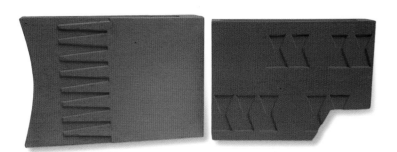

← ↑ ↓ COLOUR AND PATTERN
By introducing colour and pattern to her range
of planters, Dalwood has given them a further
design dimension.

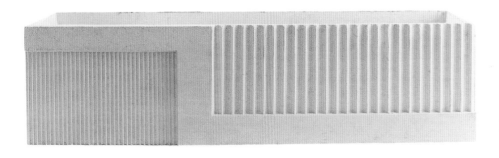

GOTTLIEB HOUSE AUSTRALIA 1994 WOOD MARSH

Wood Marsh, an Australian architectural practice based in Victoria's capital city, Melbourne, could be seen as one of the natural successors to Denton Corker Marshall (see pp 48–9). The practice's founders, Roger Wood and Randal Marsh, are relatively young and have been strongly influenced in their professional careers by the work of DCM. In addition, they have been inspired by the use of concrete in Europe during the 1960s, and later in Japan.

Both Wood and Marsh graduated from the Royal Melbourne Institute of Technology in 1983 and, along with Dale Evans, founded the design group Biltmoderne. However, the partnership with Evans ended a few years later in 1987, and it was at this point that Wood Marsh came into being.

Since then, commissions have been varied. Initially gaining recognition for a series of dramatic nightclub fit-outs, Wood Marsh have since been responsible for the design of a number of impressive domestic residences, as well as some major educational projects and an award-winning acoustic barrier for a freeway, consisting of a continuous sculptural wall of concrete running for more than 10 km (6¼ miles).

The Gottlieb House, in the Melbourne suburb of Caulfield, was designed "for a young couple with three children who had the enthusiasm to act as patrons," says Wood Marsh. The house's street-facing façade consists of a severe, windowless wall of raw concrete with a protruding, ribbed and mirrored glass box. Behind lies a much more human series of spaces, with the austere façade giving absolutely no clue as to the existence of the light and glamorous living spaces within.

The front entrance, with its dramatic and grandly curving staircase in an oval cylinder, contains a study on the ground floor and a master bedroom above. The living room is open and light, with three delineated cubes of rendered concrete on the ceiling denoting the floor plan of the three children's bedrooms above. The restrained palette of colour is complemented by the richness of the materials used including slate.

Like Tadao Ando (see pp116–17), Wood Marsh has explored the play of light and shadow on bare concrete surfaces. The interior amply demonstrates the success of contrasting the solidity of concrete with the transparency and openness of glass.

← PUBLIC FACE
This is the aspect of the dramatic Gottlieb House as it is seen from the street. All of the living spaces are hidden from public view behind the vast concrete cylinder.

→ STAIRCASE
This contemporary update of a "grand entrance staircase" made of concrete sweeps around to greet the visitor.

FOB HOUSE   JAPAN 2000   FOB ARCHITECTS

FOB is a collective, collaborative architectural practice based in Kyoto, Japan. It was founded in 1995 by Katsu Umebayashi and currently has 12 members, all architects. Projects range in scale from industrial to urban design, private houses, shops, restaurants, office buildings, and art galleries.

The practice's major initiative is FOB Homes, a design for a standardized housing system aiming to provide an alternative to the uninspiring housing kits offered by the major manufacturers, who control 99 per cent of the Japanese housing market. These manufacturers' catalogues show predominantly Western-style houses surrounded by gardens. In Japan, where space is at a premium, such houses are more likely to be ringed by a narrow yard, with windows facing directly on to their neighbour's wall. As an alternative, the FOB Homes system is based on two ideas: internal spatial continuity; and the containment of external spaces within the volume of the house. Interlocking L-shaped rooms (allowing every space to disappear around a corner) and courtyard gardens visible throughout the house give the illusion of extra space.

So far, four of these homes have been built and another 15 are at the planning stage. The houses, including all the floors, walls, and the roof, are constructed from reinforced concrete. The living room has a poured concrete base with underfloor heating. This not only makes the floor strong and easy to clean, it is also very beautiful to look at. The structure of the house consists of concrete load-bearing walls, so there are no structural elements visible. And, being made of concrete, the house remains cool in summer and stays warm throughout winter.

Associate Thomas Daniell describes the Japanese attitude toward the use of concrete; "The paradox of concrete is that its reputation as a bad material is precisely because it is such a good material. It can easily and cheaply be turned into any form you can imagine. In Japan there is a very strong post-War tradition of using *in situ* reinforced concrete for housing. Peter Eisenman has said he believes it is a post-Hiroshima psychological preparation for the 'next time'. Tadao Ando and his ilk show how beautiful bare concrete can be, and there is none of the negative associations you get in Europe for concrete in domestic architecture. In Japan, bare concrete is a seen as a very high-class material."

↑ DESIGN PRINCIPLE
The concrete floor for this combined living room and kitchen was poured in situ, as can be seen from the ripples in the surface. Clearly visible, they are intended to provide a textured effect to contrast with the smooth, white walls.

→ EXTERNAL STRUCTURE

The concrete structure demonstrates the way in which the house seems to have turned its back on the surrounding buildings.

↓ INTERIOR SPACES

The use of concrete load-bearing walls eliminates the need for supporting columns inside, thus allowing the possibility of creating light-filled and interflowing living spaces.

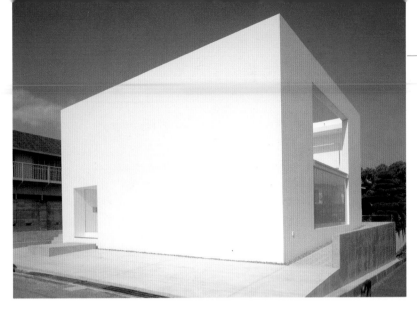

KOSHINO HOUSE   JAPAN 1979–84   TADAO ANDO

Tadao Ando has been described as the "concrete poet". Born in Osaka, Japan, in 1941, he is a self-taught architect who has assimilated and fused the best of Western Modernism with traditional Japanese architecture and Eastern philosophy. He set up his practice in 1969 and has since won all the major architectural prizes, including the Pritzker and the Gold Medal from the RIBA (Royal Insitute of British Architects).

Ando's work in concrete has been influential in encouraging others to experiment with the material. His trademark concrete walls, which have been extensively mimicked, are constructed on a block-like grid, 90 x 180 cm (35 x 70 in). Each block has six holes, the result of the moulding board screws used during construction. Many architects would have concealed them – Ando does not.

"Light and shade, cold and warm, traditional and modern, reality and dreams – these are the things you find in my work. I design beauty pure and simple, but I use the contrast for suspense and outline. Concrete is my material. It's also a universal material. It does not set limits and the designer can work it at will. But concrete is also a difficult material. Ultimately, its quality is dependent on the people who work it, on their skill and craftsmanship."

The Koshino House in Ashiya, near the city of Kobe, Japan, was constructed in two phases. Though one of Ando's earlier houses, it has been seen as one of the most influential and defining. The house initially consisted of two parallel blocks of concrete – one containing the living room, the other the bedrooms – linked by a corridor. Later, a fan-shaped extension was added to provide a studio.

The most interesting space is the living room, a double-height space in the first block constructed of Ando's trademark concrete grid. Opposite the concrete wall is a south-facing glazed wall, which allows light to flood over the material.

Ando considers that the light and the wind are architectural materials, just as much as the concrete. His concrete walls do not hide the evidence of the imperfections that are a natural part of the fabrication process and they are crafted and sometimes lacquered, so that the surface sheen offsets their actual mass: "The concrete that I use does not give the impression of solidity and weight. My concrete forms a surface, which is homogeneous, and light: the surface of the wall becomes abstract; it is transformed into nothing and approaches infinity. The existence of the wall as a substance disappears."

← → LIVING ROOM

What makes Ando's use of concrete so remarkable is the thought and attention he gives to how light will travel over the walls, and the effect of the changing seasons on the surface and texture. The skylight bands along the edge of the ceiling allow light to play across the surface of the wall, giving rise to a changing series of shadows and textures.

FLOOR | USA 1997 | TOM HURT & LAURA CARRARA-CAGNI

Tom Hurt set up in practice in 1996 after having worked for Günther Behnisch for five years. His practice, the Tom Hurt Design Office, concentrates primarily on residential architecture projects but also collaborates with other architects on commercial buildings. This project, in collaboration with Laura Carrara-Cagni, demonstrates how concrete can be utilized in a domestic interior in an altogether soft and highly decorative manner. In Europe, the use of stained and scored concrete floors is rare; in America, due to their low cost and material qualities akin to stone, the practice is more common – not only in architect-designed homes but also in speculative and builder-designed houses.

"These floors are attractive because they effectively eliminate the need to apply a top layer over the concrete floor slab," says Hurt. The top of the structural slab is used, after staining and scoring, as the finished surface. Scoring of the concrete can either become a decorative pattern or an attempt to imitate the grout joints between pieces of laid stone. Though, Hurt notes: "While the lines may suggest this, I think it is a problem if their purpose is to imitate grout. What is important and good about the scoring is that many different patterns are possible."

The possibilities of scored patterns on concrete are indeed limitless. The surface of concrete is smoother and flatter than most stone and so the scoring can create a more precise and graphic effect. Hurt feels that concrete fits in with the palette of materials used frequently in Texas, and considering the climate there, the coolness of concrete underfoot is an additional advantage.

Hurt also believes that staining concrete adds to its appeal. "Concrete is attractive because it is so simple, direct, and solid – yet it accepts some manipulation, such as the addition of stain, without losing its character. In fact, with staining a richness often emerges that would not otherwise be apparent." The stain is washed over the poured concrete after it has set – as you would mop a floor – then pigmented wax is hand-rubbed into the surface, and the floor is polished. Hurt used this technique for this project, introducing a pattern that brought scale and texture to the lower floor of the house. "I chose this pattern because it could be read in several ways, much like the patterns of Moroccan artisan carving or the designs of MC Escher."

↑ → LIVING ROOM

These views of the living room show the scored and stained concrete floor. The graphic pattern can be read in several ways, and from several different directions. A completely level surface allows great precision in pattern-making.

BATTERSEA FLAT   UK 1999 | PATEL TAYLOR

Pankaj Patel and Andrew Taylor set up in practice in 1989 while both were teaching at the Bartlett School of Architecture in London. Their early reputation came as a result of success in a number of international competitions, and the practice has since undertaken a broad range of building types, from sensitive conversions, public buildings, and crafted homes to large environmental projects.

A shell covering an area of 325 sq m (3,500 sq ft) and 5 m (16½ ft) high, with brick walls, iron columns, and a rough, concrete floor formed the setting for this first-floor loft apartment in a former Victorian tobacco warehouse in London's Battersea.

The client's brief was for substantial accommodation, including three bedrooms and bathrooms, that retained the unique volume and essence of the space. Patel Taylor, therefore, decided to leave the western side of the shell as open as possible, allowing natural light and views out to three aspects, while incorporating the more private areas into the eastern side. The living, dining, and kitchen spaces flow into each other, defined only by the use of floating ceilings, screens, and shutters as well as changing floor materials.

A rich and varied palette of materials was employed, including French and English oak, iroko, three types of limestone, blue steel plate, sand-blasted glass, stainless steel, and leather. A zig-zagging concrete wall, cast in situ, created a "weight" and focus to the living areas. The wall also separates the private and public areas, leading from the entrance into the key spaces.

The exposed moulding board screw marks in the concrete express the method of construction, giving it a crafted quality. Imperfections, such as blow holes and colour variations, are accepted, in the same way as knots in wood or veins in natural stone. Associate Mike Kaner explains: "Much time was spent and many samples made to perfect the finish, colour, and texture. Variables in the equation, such as casting temperature, cement and aggregate types and percentages, type of formwork, and the amount of vibration, lead to what is almost a recipe – like baking a complex cake."

One of the qualities of concrete is its neutrality – its ability to mix with and enhance other materials without clashing with them or making the whole seem fussy or over-designed. Concrete is used frequently as a canvas on to which other materials can effectively be applied to accentuate their contrasting properties.

↑ → DEMARCATING SPACE

Although the living, dining, and kitchen areas all flow into one another, the concrete wall, changing floor materials, and screens effectively signal the private and public areas of the living space.

COLOURED CONCRETE

MEXICO | LUIS BARRAGAN

In the words of the Mexican essayist and poet Octavio Paz, speaking of his contemporary: "Luis Barragán is a quiet, solitary artist, who has lived far removed from the ideological factions and the hypnotic power of committed art." Barragán was born in 1902 and before his death in 1988 he became widely recognized as one of the most influential Mexican architects.

An engineer by training, Barragán is famed for his use of colour, light, and space in his dramatic yet simple houses and gardens, and through his work he has exerted a powerful influence on the way in which utilitarian materials are regarded in the context of the domestic interior. "The lessons to be learned from the unassuming architecture of the villages and provincial towns of my country have been a permanent source of inspiration for me," wrote Barragán. And, indeed, it was adobe, render, local stone and concrete that formed the rough canvas for his work. His favourite materials, however, were water and light, and his obsession was the effect that he could achieve with them.

After completing a tour taking in Europe and North Africa in 1920, the young Barragán found himself deeply impressed by the casbahs, the Moorish architecture and courtyards, and the Mediterranean colours he found in the region. On his return home to Mexico, Barragán initially and, it must be said, rather uncomfortably embarked on a series of designs in the International modern style of the Swiss-born architect Le Corbusier, after seeing his L'Esprit Nouveau pavilion at the Exposition des Arts Décoratif, in Paris. On a later European visit, Barragán met Ferdinand Bac, whose designs for gardens and writings had a profound influence on the architect.

During this period in his career, Barragán adopted modern building techniques. These included the use of reinforced concrete for roofs though, as his own distinctive style became more defined, he abandoned this approach, turning instead to more traditional construction methods in which he replaced concrete with wooden roofing beams. Finding in the 1950s his own unique combination of Modernism and Regionalism, he developed a palette of dramatic colours, shadows, and vistas. He believed that: "Colour is a complement to architecture. It seems to widen or narrow a space. It is also helpful in adding that magic touch that a space requires."

↑ SATELLITE TOWERS
Built in Mexico City by Luis Barragán (1957), the shuttering left by the formwork can be clearly seen in the Satellite City Towers. This is a deliberate visual statement on the painted surface of the towers.

→ INDOOR POOL
Barragán describes the indoor pool in the Francisco Gilardi House (1976): "The column in the middle of the pool goes against the rules, but it needed to be there in order to bring another colour to the composition."

Barragán made his spaces emotive and poetic with a Latin sensibility. The wall was paramount in his compositions. "All architecture that does not express serenity fails in its spiritual mission. Thus it has been a mistake to abandon the shelter of walls for the inclemency of large areas of glass. Corners, wall height, gardens and textures. I use them all in order to demonstrate three things: time, place, and sensation." Barragán had the advantage of coming from a wealthy family background and, therefore, had the luxury of often acting as his own client or developer. In this way, external financial or client pressures rarely compromised his architectural vision.

The only Barragán projects that are obviously of concrete are the Satellite Towers in Mexico City, built in 1957, and the Commerce Tower in Monterrey, Mexico, which was completed in 1977. The Satellite Towers exhibit the influence of Barragán's design collaborator on the project, Mathais Goeritz, a sculptor well known for his work in concrete. The project consists of a group of five towers, varying between 34 and 57 m (110 and 190 ft) in height, and standing in the middle of a motorway where they form a symbolic entrance to Ciudad Satellite, a suburb of Mexico City.

Originally painted in a range of bright, primary hues, the colours of the Satellite Towers were later changed by Barragán to the more muted tones of terracotta orange. After that he changed his mind again and reverted to the primary colours that he had originally planned for. Barragán consulted the artist Jesus "Chucho" Reyes, who selected the colours for the towers. Barragán claimed that his inspiration for the work were in fact the towers of San Gimignano in Italy.

One of my favourite images of concrete is a photograph of a workman, balanced precariously, painting with a large, wide brush the side of one of the Satellite Towers. In a single stroke of the brush he can be seen transforming the tower from grey to a warm red. Barragán's use of colour on concrete is inspirational. The architect Louis Kahn, with whom Barragán had collaborated on the central court of the Salk Institute, said: "The architecture of Barragán is timeless. It could have been constructed a hundred years ago or a hundred years from now."

↑ → CHANGING COLOURS
Interior and exterior views of the Antonio Gálvez House (1955). The way in which the shadow moves across the wall transforms the colour throughout the day from shocking pink to rose.

UTILITY

Utility and utilitarianism – the practical usefulness rather than the aesthetic quality of concrete has long been seen as being one of the materials primary advantages, from its earliest use as a construction element for the foundations for buildings, and as one of the hidden elements of construction.

Concrete's constituent parts – sand, stone chippings or pebbles, cement, and water – are all individually inexpensive elements, a fact which has undoubtedly led many people to believe that the material could never be a "proper" material in its own right for architecture. But the fact is that concrete isn't cheap – the expense that is associated with producing high-quality concrete, which can often be more than the cost of using stone or wood, lies in the skill and the labour involved.

While some architects and designers strive to manufacture concrete with the smoothest-possible, silk-like finish, others are more attracted by the roughness and the utilitarian nature of lower-quality concrete; such concrete often incorporates the larger grades of aggregate and this is the construction material that often forms the bones of utility or industrial buildings such as warehouses, factories, and offices.

The lifestyle trend toward loft living, seen in many domestic schemes over the last few years for revitalizing city centres and other former industrial environments, has literally exposed concrete within the domestic environment. It is a trend which perhaps has a late 20th-century equivalent in the enthusiasm for stripping back the paint from pine, as part of the renovation process of Victorian and Georgian homes, which was an extremely popular practice in the 1970s and 1980s. It illustrates many of the same processes and highlights many similar problems and misconceptions. The pine used in these speculative and low-quality early estates was very poor and the wood was rarely matched because it was expected that it would be painted or heavily stained and, therefore, never seen by the homeowner in its raw state. Shutters, doors, floors, and balustrades that have been stripped in a frenzy of so-called "restoration" often consist of mismatched and oddly coloured panels, the sight of which would undoubtedly make

← LOFT APARTMENT
An Oliver Heath interior. The concrete floor is exposed in this "original" loft. Exposed steel girders and columns, and concrete floors and ceilings typify the industrial loft aesthetic.

→ CHURCH OF THE LIGHT
An interior view of Tadao Ando's Church of the Light, Osaka, Japan (1987–9). The simplicity of the concrete, its lack of artifice, helps to encourage a spiritual environment.

any self-respecting Victorian builder turn in his grave. But this trend has developed into the fashion for wooden floors generally and the widespread use of predominantly unpainted, waxed wood, rather than timber that has been heavily varnished and stained. And the same process can be detected in the evolution of concrete within the domestic interior

The early "real-loft" conversions in old industrial buildings were such a radical departure from traditional apartment interior design because, for the first time, concrete columns and soffits were made into a "feature", which made such an impact that they started a trend for the use of exposed concrete in loft apartments. And, of course, if concrete was not already present in the original structure of the building, then it could always be added in the shape of baths, floors, dividing walls, kitchen worktops, and so on, in order to complete the "loft aesthetic".

Standard, non-domestic components – usually hard landscaping materials such as paving slabs, bollards, and breeze blocks – were also occasionally utilized to create this tough, urban interior, at a time when designed concrete artefacts were most likely to be found in art galleries. Then, products intended specifically for the home were not readily available in the marketplace.

This trend has, however, seeped further afield and is now often to be found as a part of the non-loft domestic interior. But the rough, utilitarian aspect of concrete – which, in truth, can be quite difficult to live with – has disappeared and a far more sophisticated and "crafted" approach has taken over.

Concrete's utility has been replaced by preciousness, the material is now given the same consideration as "luxury" materials such as granite or marble. Exposed aggregate and large aggregate concrete does not fit in with the current fair-faced aesthetic and, therefore, there are not many examples included in this book. But fashions change, and so fashions in the appearance of concrete will change, too.

Often in the domestic environment it is when concrete is used simply that it is most successful. When concrete is employed with other building materials, acting more as a canvas or backdrop rather than shouting out as the main element, that concrete finds a general acceptance.

Part of the attraction of using concrete, from the designers' point of view in particular, lies in the fact that it is relatively easy material to use. To make concrete, you basically follow a recipe; the proportions of "ingredients" are based upon the desired results, and the designer can add seasoning to their own personal taste.

Concrete isn't therefore a daunting material to tackle; the results depend 100 per cent on the creativity of the maker, so it is an extremely responsive material. Unlike marble or stone, its constituent elements are basically cheap, which therefore tends to encourage experimentation. It is a material which will allow the incorporation of unusual aggregates, pigments, and other materials with very little fuss. This utility, combined with its plasticity has made concrete a perfect material for designers and artists. For concrete can be both poetic and immensely practical.

↓ FLOORING

A simple concrete floor incorporating an underfloor heating system creates a sensuous and tactile surface.

→ SIMPLE SCREENING

An interior view of a house in Hampstead, London designed by Brian Housden showing the exposed concrete frame. The dining area has been screened off quite simply using a pink hospital curtain.

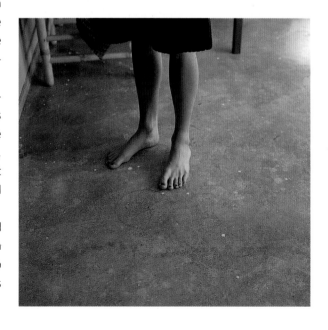

FUSION BOXES & SINK

DENMARK 2000 | REBECCA UTH

Rebecca Uth is an industrial designer based in Copenhagen, Denmark, and is a graduate of The Danish School of Design. She has been responsible for the design of a range of innovative concrete tables that can be described as blurring the boundaries between design and art. Of all of her other designs, the sink has the most immediately obvious function and comprises a large, combined fibreglass-reinforced concrete sink and drainer, where the tap splashes water directly on to a non-recessed surface. As Uth explains: "The kitchen is the centre of water circulation in a house. Here the water becomes visible and creates shape when meeting the tabletop and the sink."

Her Fusion Boxes are a range of cubes that fuse different functional elements together into one object. In one Fusion Box, a table and a light are fused into one, in other Boxes a table and a rug; and a table and plate. All of her tables are made of fibreglass-reinforced concrete cubes.

"I make objects that have an air of a manifesto and which challenge the sensuous, rational, retentive, and emotional abilities of the human being. The objects illustrate and emphasize the rituals of everyday life. They make us conscious of our relationship with the objects and materials that surround us."

Uth continues: "The common denominator for the projects is that they deal with our time – the ways in which we live and those objects that surround us in our daily lives in our homes. The design objectives are influenced by the Nordic design tradition and are, furthermore, characterized by simplicity of the form, materials, and aesthetics."

Uth's work is startling in the way that it contrasts concrete with other materials. The austerity of the concrete in the sink project makes the water more visible, and, for the Fusion Boxes, it heightens the texture and pattern of the rug, the warmth and cosiness of the red velvet, and the scale and fragility of the light.

→ SINK

Water splashes over the sealed surface of the concrete sink top, before being directed into the bowl.

↑ → FUSION BOXES

Two entirely different treatments of a concrete cube. The carpet makes the concrete appear to be comfortable, while the red velvet renders it warm and luxurious.

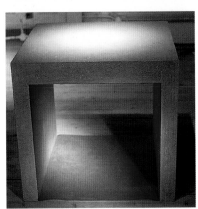

↑ ↓ FUSION BOXES

Uth humorously combines a table and a dog bowl in the above Fusion Box. The table and light Fusion Box (below) is more artwork than practical design.

BOOKSHELVES FRANCE 2000 FRANCESCO PASSANITI

The multi-faceted Italian Franceso Passaniti is not only a talented artist and an architect, he is also a sculptor who has chosen concrete as his preferred material. According to the journalist Francesca Torre: "Passaniti speaks of concrete as something entirely natural, a mineral like any other, using such terms as 'rough and stone-like' or 'worn smooth by time' to describe its textures. The agelessness and, above all, the tactile sensitivity of concrete seem to fascinate him."

"Concrete preserves the marks and imprints we leave on it with extraordinary accuracy," Passaniti eloquently elaborates on the subject of his work", so I take a great deal of trouble over the pebbles, sands, additives, and pigments of my concrete mixes. They are like my signature, locked forever into the material."

When commissioned by journalist Simonetta Greggio to redesign a tiny Parisian apartment, all of Passaniti's creative flare was brought to bear – when working with a total floor area of a mere 58 sq m (625 sq ft), you cannot afford to waste space with dead areas of internal walls.

Bearing in mind his client's need for separate living and sleeping areas, Passaniti designed open concrete bookshelves that perform not only as a convenient storage and display unit, but also effectively divide one room into two.

This was both a pragmatic and an elegant solution to making the most of the apartment's limited resources. Introducing a solid wall would have broken up an already small space and made the sleeping area too dark and very unappealing, whereas the open design of the bookcase-cum-room divider allows light to flow between the spaces virtually unhindered.

The architect's love of concrete can be seen in many other aspects of the apartment. For example, the bed, at the flick of a switch, neatly folds itself into the wall, thus freeing-up the space to be used as a writing area, with the concrete bedside table converting into a desk. And in the bathroom, Passaniti had used a mixture of anthracite grey and red-pigmented concrete to create a stylishly dramatic yet intimate space.

→ ROOM DIVIDER

The bold shelving here separates the bedroom area from the main living space. It is a solid barrier, yet allows light to filter through. The chunkiness and the solidity of the material is used to great effect.

RECORD DECK UK 1987 RON ARAD

Though an early project by Ron Arad, Professor of Product Design at the Royal College of Art, London, the concrete stereo has been highly influential, inspiring other designers to look at the possibilities of concrete, and not the perfect, fair-faced type either.

The architecture and design critic Deyan Sudjic wrote that Arad's concrete stereo shattered the preconception of hi-fi as a precision instrument, "It is neither well-mannered nor discreet. Even today it is a seriously subversive, even transgressive object ... The heat sink emerges from the amplifier's petrified stomah, like some half-digested fish supper. The vulnerability of the vinyl disc and of the fragile diamond-tipped stylus make for a teeth-jarring contrast with the ragged roughness of raw concrete and rusty-looking steel."

The stereo was inspired by the building work Arad saw around him in London. The electronics were wrapped in plastic, then covered with quick-setting concrete. When set, he hammered away with a chisel to reveal the guts of the product. Though not intended to be the best in terms of sound quality, the blurring of the boundary between art and design proved that hi-fi design could, in fact, be different. It is a product that now fetches art-style prices at auction.

Arad went on to design other concrete pieces, such as The Tree Light and a concrete-topped table. He also produced designs for fashion icon John-Paul Gaultier's shop in London in 1986, with concrete figures supporting the clothes rails.

In his own shop, One Off, railway sleepers formed the treads of a staircase cantilevering out from a concrete wall. Arad's experiments with concrete didn't last, as he explains: "There was no need to be overproductive ... I looked at concrete because I was building my shop and had a lot of it around. I didn't think it was pointing the way forward." He then turned to other materials, initially steel and then plastic. Arad's fascination with the potential of different materials has seen his designs develop from one-offs into mass-production, influencing a generation of consumers and designers.

→ RON ARAD'S STEREO
The record deck was part of a series produced by Ron Arad when his highly influential shop, One Off, was open in London's Covent Garden.

BOLLARDS COFFEE TABLE UK 1999 | WILLIAM WARREN

Although William Warren studied silversmithing at the Royal College of Art in London, he has since gone on to design in a range of scales and different materials, encompassing both stainless-steel (for cutlery) and concrete (for dining tables). He founded Mod Cons in 1998 and now designs interiors, furnishings, commissioned furniture, and lighting. His Bollards coffee table, which he designed in conjunction with Toby Hatchett, forms part of an urban range of furniture that expresses something of the inner-city lifestyle and environment.

"The legs are," says Warren, "cast directly from a bollard I found in the street. I did it at night, armed with a box, a bucket of water, plaster of Paris, and a tub of Vaseline. I was very careful not to get caught rubbing Vaseline on to a bollard in the middle of Peckham at night, as I reasoned that this was an act that I could not easily explain away."

Warren could not use real bollards for the legs as they were too tall, especially when you take into account that more than 46 cm (18 in) of a bollard is actually embedded in the ground. In addition, the finish was different – Warren wanted to achieve a more exposed aggregate finish, so before the concrete was completely dry he attacked the surface with a wire brush to remove the top layer of concrete.

The other furniture he has designed in this range includes a bed called "Sleeping Rough" – based on a park bench but with a seat deep enough to hold a double mattress – and a stool printed with double yellow lines to discourage it being sat on. Another concrete product he has designed is "Your umbrella sleeps with the fishes" – an umbrella stand consisting of a pair of wellington boots sunk in a cube of concrete. As Warren explains, with more than a touch of irony: "I designed this when I was looking into *incidental crafts*. By this I mean the situation when people produce lovely, pragmatic solutions to problems without realizing they are even doing it. Whether there ever was an occasion when a victim had his feet cast in concrete before being thrown in the water or not, it is still a great idea. My version implies that the victim has long since rotted away, thus demonstrating the longevity of the material. The first prototype is still in the river Thames in London, under Blackfriars Bridge, and it can sometimes still be seen at very low tide."

→ COFFEE TABLE
The use of an urban street setting to display the table is intended to emphasize its design heritage.

DETAILS UK 2000 TOTEM DESIGN

Totem is a group of architectural designers who combine strong design skills with production expertise. They specialize in domestic interiors, bars, and restaurants, and much of their work is executed in concrete. Early projects included concrete kitchen worktops, which often incorporated features that exploited the flexibility of the medium, such as inserting wooden chopping boards into concrete surfaces or scooping out spaces for waste disposals.

Ian Hume from Totem has had, unlike many architects, years of practical experience with concrete, partly because he studied furniture design as well as architecture, and so has developed hands-on experience of experimenting and making. Trial and error have made him something of an expert, and he has developed his own secret recipes and techniques. Hume believes that concrete is an "honest material", and he admires it for both its structural potential and its flexibility: "It is the only material that is so versatile, particularly in its ability to have other elements inserted in it, such as wood, glass, or even MDF. Though surprisingly delicate, it is also flexible and strong and can be cast in almost any shape, so the possibilities are very exciting. It is the most challenging of materials."

The smooth, polished quality of his concrete surfaces and their crisp edges are the result of years of practice and experience. Hume believes that concrete is best used on a chunky, monolithic scale, to demonstrate its structural strength. For a kitchen project in a loft apartment, Hume incorporated a concrete wine rack as a support for a cantilevered worktop. Cast on the floor, it was lifted into place with sunken lights installed behind it. Its *objet trouvé* industrial form fits well with the apartment aesthetic, and its size and strength enable it to take some of the weight of the worktop.

Hume did not consider designing this wine rack in any material other than concrete. For Hume, the aim is "to create a balance and contrast between light and space, void and mass", achieved by mixing concrete with a palette of other materials, such as wood and glass, to keep a balance. In the same apartment project he combined concrete with stainless-steel electrical sockets and with wood, suspending a concrete step over a wooden floor.

The only negative aspect associated with using concrete in a domestic interior that Hume can think of is culinary. "Balsamic vinegar is the enemy of concrete; spills can leave a terrible stain."

↑ ELECTRICAL SOCKET

A stainless-steel electrical plug socket, of a type more commonly found in a laboratory setting, has been sunk into the concrete to emphasize the industrial aesthetic of the worktop. The smoothness of the steel contrasts with the roughness of the concrete.

→ BOTTLE RACK

Though designed specifically for the loft apartment project, this wine rack has the slightly battered appearance of a found, reclaimed object with an industrial past. The holes can either be filled with bottles or left empty to act as sculptural lights.

→ → STEPS

Resting on a wooden plinth, this concrete stepping stone appears to hover above the wooden floor — an effect achieved by lighting it from below. Here, a small, concrete plank is used as a single element to transform an otherwise uninteresting, simple step into an eye-catching feature.

BENCHES UK 2000 FIELD DAY

Penny Howarth, a graphic designer who has also studied sculpture and landscape architecture, established her company, Field Day, in 1999. Field Day presents a new approach to the modern exterior space, producing moveable, urban garden installations that can also be successfully transferred into the domestic interior. In order to keep product lines fresh and new ideas flowing through, the company keeps manufacturing runs short and as well as introducing new ideas on a regular basis, Howarth also undertakes one-offs and individual private projects. "My inspiration comes primarily from big landscapes and art, and I like to bring elements from these sources into a smaller, more urban context," says Howarth.

Howarth likes to blur the boundaries between the interior and the exterior by incorporating into her designs materials that are usually associated with outdoor use only. One of the materials she uses in this way is concrete, which she feels gives the pieces a more substantial and rugged quality. As Howarth notes: "I love the way that concrete looks; it has a fabulous utilitarian quality that you simply don't get with stone, and its surface appearance changes according to the ambient weather conditions. However, the endless variables involved in its manufacture can be a headache. And so, too, can its transportation: on the one hand, it is heavy while, on the other, it wants to be treated delicately."

Among the pieces that Howarth designs are Field Boxes. These are made of precast, unreinforced, grey concrete with a concealed base to raise them slightly off the ground. Also in her range is a Grass Bench. This looks best when simply planted with grass or camomile. Like the Field Boxes, it is made of precast, grey concrete, but the bench is reinforced and contains a cavity to house the soil and plants. A water pipe is laid into the soil when planting up the bench to concentrate the watering just below the surface of the soil. This not only puts the water where it is most needed by the plants, so reducing losses due to evaporation, it also lessens the likelihood of users getting wet when they sit on it.

Howarth is on the point of launching a new range of products, including a series of very large panoramic light boxes containing "borrowed landscapes" to act as gardens views for homes that don't have gardens. In addition, she is creating coloured cast-plastic rocks and rockface wall hangings.

↑ FIELD BOXES
The concrete planters work particularly well when they are clustered together and then filled with contrasting plant forms.

→ ↓ BENCHES

Two versions of the concrete bench can be seen here. Like the planters, the benches are made of precast concrete and have an arrangement of pipes to aid watering, and drainage to keep users dry when they sit on them.

KITCHEN | UK 2000 | HOUSE OF S & N

House of S & N consists of two partners, Steven Separovich and Tina Horden. Separovich was born in Adelaide, Australia, and studied architecture and interior design before moving to England in 1995. Horden was born in Hamburg, Germany, and studied architecture at the University of Westminster and the Royal College of Art, both in London. They met while working for the same practice and formed House of S & N in 1997. As well as domestic projects they have recently completed a restaurant in Hampstead, north London.

With the commission pictured here, the clients – one an American, the other British – both design-conscious, were very involved. One of them is professionally involved in cooking and the other in the theatre, so the kitchen was designed to become the dramatic focal point of the house. S & N's approach was to play on the implied contrast between functionality and spatial drama by combining opposing elements – solidity versus transparency, rough versus smooth, light versus dark. Pairing seemingly utilitarian materials, such as bead-blasted stainless steel and concrete surfaces, with rich walnut and refined, dark-blue slate helps to give the space a strong identity. The clean, contemporary lines of the kitchen ele-

ments also provide an intentionally stark contrast with the period features of the house, establishing a clear delineation between old and new. The added elements are a central food-preparation unit, wall units with open shelving, a cantilevered window bench, and a central cooking unit with tall cupboards. The theatrical aspect of the kitchen proposal is evident in the thick, L-shaped, concrete central unit, which is seemingly supported on a sheet of illuminated glass.

S & N believe that concrete was the only material suitable for realizing their idea, but the clients needed persuading. As the clients themselves have reported: "When S & N first suggested concrete, images of Lasdun's grey shutter-boarded pillboxes floated before use. We had wanted work surfaces with the richness of limestone, the texture of sandstone, and a durability that neither could offer. There is of course a price to pay. Compared with the simplicity of having prefabricated worktops shipped in and fitted in a day, one must gives one's space over to a process that takes several weeks of forming, casting, sanding, and polishing. This is not a process for the fainthearted, but the results are tangible and the rewards are considerable."

← CONCRETE WORKTOP
A view of the central preparation area of the kitchen, with a concrete worktop encasing the shelving and white goods below.

→ SINK
A detail of the sink area worktop, in pale-coloured concrete crafted by Kayode Lipede (see also pp 78–9). The glass splash back is illuminated from behind to produce a warm glow.

HUDSON HOUSE IRELAND 1998 O'DONNELL AND TUOMEY

Sheila O'Donnell and John Tuomey set up in practice in 1988 and since then have developed a reputation for their cultural and educational buildings, including the Irish Film Centre, National Photography Centre in Ireland and a multi-denominational school.

This project, for a new build house in Navan, Ireland, presented them with a challenge. The site was inaccessible and, being a long narrow back garden with a restaurant in front, did not appear to be an obvious place to build. The restaurant owners had been living over their business, and now they wanted to move out into the garden to allow the restaurant to expand upstairs. They had taken over a roofless concrete shell of a backyard workshop as a sheltered space in which to escape the heat of the kitchen.

"As we started sketching to look for a response to the unusual problems confronting us, we realized that the solution was implicit in the situation and that we could build the house by building the site," says John Tuomey.

The house is organized in plan and section around three courtyards placed between the existing house and its back garden. The living space and the bedroom tower are positioned on either side of the footprint of the former workshop. Retaining walls hold back the higher level neighbours' gardens on each side of the plot. Glazed doors connect the living and courtyard spaces, and the flagstone floor also links the two. Concrete steps lead from the courtyard level to the existing raised garden at the rear.

The house is built of concrete lined internally with plasterboard and plywood. The concrete shell was completed in just six weeks, but due to contractual complications the shell stood empty for a few weeks, looking like a strange modern ruin or sculpture. Large wooden-framed windows alleviate the mass of the fair-faced concrete. The exterior woodwork of untreated iroke will weather to a silvery grey to blend in with the concrete over time. As Tuomey explains: "Concrete defines the outer shell, retaining walls, and structural form … Casting the structure in concrete allowed us to create three kinds of space out of a single, monolithic material. The cave, the courtyard, and the tower are the constituent elements of the house excavated from the existing conditions of the site."

O'Donnell and Tuomey are now currently working on a second concrete house project.

← STAIRWAY

An exposed concrete wall flanks the stairway. The use of concrete in the interior of the house has been limited to the main structural elements, referring to the exterior concrete shell.

→ CONCRETE AND WOOD

An external detail showing a wooden window shutter. When new, the untreated iroke panelling contrasts with the concrete; over time, however, it will weather to match perfectly in colour.

LOFT & EXTENSION

Block Architecture is a young practice based in London, its two partners – Zoe Smith and Graeme Williamson – having graduated only in 1997. The practice relies on a mixture of commercial and residential work, with commissions in both London and New York, as well as a series of self-initiated projects motivated by the pair's desire to explore new ways of reusing residual urban space.

In the two projects shown here, Block Architecture has utilized concrete in very different ways. The aim for the loft interior was to keep the long concrete shell as open-plan as possible. The client's preference was for a raw look, less slick than most contemporary loft conversions. The idea was to keep the original structure exposed and to use materials that would wear and mellow with the interior. Their unusual solution for the bathroom was to mount it on an exposed concrete plinth. The raised slab defines the bathroom and incorporates a concrete shower tray. To the left of the bath lies the kitchen area, also running along the wall, where the same concrete finish has been used for the work surface, forming an effective contrast with the stainless-steel sink and black steel splashback.

The new-build extension is a lean-to structure supported by a concrete wall, which was cast in situ using pronounced formwork. The shuttering banding is clearly visible on the surface of the concrete, and the initial impression is that the wall is constructed from strips of wood. As Graeme Williamson explains: "We used the roughest grade of shuttering possible, so rough in fact that some of the shuttering wood is still embedded in the concrete. So the wall looks like it needs a shave."

The wall divides the kitchen from the external cooking area, and supports both a barbecue and ledge, also cast from concrete, for cooking materials and utensils. The exterior decking is red cedar, which is weathering to a shade of grey to match the concrete wall.

Like many young architects in Britain, Smith and Williamson have been influenced by the use of concrete in such buildings as the South Bank complex in London. At present, they are using concrete for a project in New York, where the fabrication of a concrete bath, shower, and work surface was made possible by the use of a secret composition of super-light aggregates. "Concrete technology is changing," notes Williamson, "making people who have rejected the material in the past look at it again with fresh eyes."

↑ LOFT & KITCHEN CONVERSION
Instead of creating a separate bathroom, the bath and shower area was placed in the centre of the wall on a floating, polished concrete slab, its utilitarian nature emphasized by the half-painted brick wall behind and the simple white tiles.

→ NEW-BUILD EXTENSION
The shuttering of the formwork used for the cast concrete wall was selected to be the same width as the decking in order to emphasize the relationship between the wall and floor.

BYRNE HOUSE   USA 1999   WILL BRUDER

Will Bruder is an artist/architect who has worked from his desert studio in New River, Arizona, for the past 25 years. Born in Milwaukee, Wisconsin, in 1946, Bruder earned a BA in sculpture and is a self-trained architect. In addition to his formal education, he was apprenticed under Paolo Soleri and Gunnar Birkerts and has experience in carpentry, masonry, and metal work.

The concept for the Byrne Residence in Scottsdale, Arizona, was to "create a metaphorical series of abstract 'canyon walls' and spaces that emerge as metaphoric geological gestures from the natural desert site." The building's functional needs occur on two levels that integrate into the site's natural slope. The angular orientation of the structure, which is parallel to the site's natural contours, enhances the home's fit with the land and optimizes the views from all the major main-level living spaces.

The tilted, non-vertical orientation of the exposed concrete-block "canyon walls" serves further to frame the site's dramatic desert vistas. The finished effect Bruder wanted to achieve was for the walls to look as if they had been magically folded up from the surface of the landscape.

To complement and contrast with the dominant concrete walls, elements of the wall and fascia are clad in naturally patinated copper and acid-etched galvanized metal. These materials, with their purple/bronze and pewter-grey tones, blend well with the natural landscape and the rustic concrete.

Bruder describes the background to the project: "Carol and Bill Byrne moved to the desert from an old colonial house in New Jersey. Carol is a fabric colourist and Bill is a wood framing contractor who is now vice-president of a construction company. Their new desert house was conceived as a geological artifact on a site where the land has been lifted and shifted by time, wind, and cataclysmic events. The architecture seeks to explore those realities. The simple forms emerge stealth-like from the landscape. Raked concrete, blue-black etched copper, and the poetry of the meeting of building and landscape speak about simplicity. We came to the site one day to find Bill down on all fours with golf balls. He was sure the floors were not level but could not get the balls to roll. The way that light dances across the walls and the floor is discovered through movement from dawn to dusk. The house amplifies nature's subtlety."

↑ A MARRIAGE OF CONCEPTS
Craftsmanlike in his concern for detail and building process, his architecture is sculptural in its unique choreography of space, movement, materials, and light.

→ ENTRANCE
The entry is a passage into a "canyon" that begins the choreography of movement and light. The slope of the land is embodied in the energy of the raking walls.

CRESCENT HOUSE

UK 1997 | KEN SHUTTLEWORTH

This house, by the architect Ken Shuttleworth, a partner in the world-famous practice of Foster and Partners, was designed for his own family. The brief was demanding:

"It must be warm in winter, yet not get too hot in summer; it has to be environmentally friendly and low maintenance; it has to be 'low tech' without complex controls. In addition, all plumbing and wiring has to be accessible, not buried in walls or floors. It needs areas that are accessible to wheelchair users. All walls are to be white. It should have a generous hall and front door and a large fireplace as a focal point. It should be bathed in light and the overall feel should be spacious and airy, yet utilitarian and functional. It should not be lavish, profligate or precious. It has to be finished for Christmas lunch 1997." Quite a challenge.

The plan of the house consists of two parallel crescents, a design rooted strongly in its location and historically, too, since Wiltshire is a county rich is ancient stone circles and earthworks. The design concept creates two very distinct sides. To the northwest, the house presents a solid, convex wall, shutting out a nearby road, neighbouring homes, and the wind to provide more privacy. In this crescent are the family spaces, such as the bedrooms and bathrooms, with skylights for day-time illumination and starry nights.

The house opens up on the southeast with a concave crescent of clear glass embracing the sun and the best views, drawing them into the main living space. Here, the kitchen, dining area, and play area for the family's two children are located. Full-height glass allows maximum visual contact with the landscape.

The decision to build the house from concrete was aided by the presence of a concrete plant directly across the road from the site. Minimal transportation would be involved and Shuttleworth, therefore, decided to make maximum use of this very local resource. In addition, recycled fill material below the slabs and second-hand timber from the previous house on the site (which was demolished) were used for the formwork. The concrete structure with its masonry infill provides a very high thermal capacity, acting as a heat store and so reducing the rate of temperature fluctuations.

There are no fancy designer taps or luxurious materials. The design emphasizes lightness and space, details and decoration are kept to a minimum to reduce distraction from the views and space.

↓ CORRIDORS

High windows flood the crescent-shaped corridors in light without compromising the family's privacy. In line with the initial brief, the style is simple, utilitarian, and airy, yet it remains functional and welcoming.

→ BATHROOM

The big bath and long sink were constructed of concrete primarily because it was a cheap option. It helped not only to keep the scheme within tight budget constraints but also to maintain the intrinsic simplicity of the overall design.

↓ ENTRANCE

The graceful curve of the convex crescent wall heightens the sense of arrival and anticipation of the entrance, with the position of the door being deliberately obscured.

GLOSSARY

Additives Concrete additives are sometimes used to affect the workability, setting, or frost resistance of concrete.

Agents Fine-grain substances that modify specific properties of the concrete. They are primarily related to the workability of new concrete, and the strength and density of the material after hardening.

Aggregate Usually gravel or crushed stone, forming 50%–80% of the volume of concrete. It is added to a binding agent (see cement) with water and sand.

Blitzcrete Colourful aggregates such as brick fragments are used to produce a concrete called "Blitzcrete". Named by architect John Outram after the concrete he made using debris found from World War II bomb sites.

Cement The binding agent combines with sand, water, and aggregate, to create concrete. The terms "cement" and "concrete" are often used interchangeably, but cement is not a structural material.

Cinder or clinker block A cheap lightweight precast concrete block using clinker (fused ash) as an aggregate.

Concrete cancer Common name for alkali-silica reaction, caused by alkalis in the cement reacting with silica in the aggregate. Water can then seep in, crack the concrete, and eventually rust the steel reinforcement.

↑ KITCHEN CONSTRUCTION
Stages in the construction of a monolithic reinforced concrete worktop cast in situ. The steel reinforcement is clearly visible, as is the formwork around the edges of the benchtop and the inserts used to leave gaps for the sink, electrical outlets, and appliances. The concrete wine rack was cast separately and inserted under the finished bench.

↑ → KITCHEN
The smooth, continuous surfaces of the finished kitchen. The lightweight storage unit hanging from an existing steel beam contrasts with the heaviness of the bench and incorporates recessed down lights to light the work surface.

Curing The process of preventing fresh concrete from drying to minimize cracking and give it time to strengthen.

Ferro-concrete An obsolete term for reinforced concrete.

Formwork Temporary structure or mould into which newly mixed concrete is poured. It may be constructed of glass fibre, plastic, rubber, steel, or timber. When removed, it leaves an impression on the surface of the concrete.

In situ concrete Concrete which is made on site (cast in place) rather than made and transported to the site (see precast concrete). Most worktops, baths, and stairs are cast in situ as it can be very difficult to precast and transport large pieces. Casting in situ is more expensive and messy but the results are unique.

Perlite An expanded volcanic glass used as an aggregate in the production of lightweight concrete.

Precast concrete Concrete that has been set off-site in moulds, and which are transported to the site for assembly.

Prestressed concrete Concrete in which a prestressed steel cable has been placed during manufacture to induce permanent internal stresses, permitting longer spans than reinforced concrete will allow.

Post-tensioned concrete Concrete in which high-strength steel tendons, in combination with reinforcement bars, are embedded into the concrete. When the concrete has dried, the tendons are stretched to induce a permanent compression load on the concrete. The system allows engineers to design shallower structural floors and beams with increased load capacity.

Reinforced concrete Concrete with a net of steel bars embedded in it to overcome its weakness in tension, therefore increasing its loadbearing capacity.

Shotcrete A rough, sprayed concrete finish. From a distance, good shotcrete can resemble suede or a thick pile carpet. The concrete is retarded to prevent it blocking in the spray gun.

Thermal capacity Concrete's thermal capacity: the ability to absorb heat from the sun during the day and radiate it back into the interior at night, which reduces energy consumption in buildings and ensures a relatively constant temperature.

INFORMATION

National Concrete organizations can usually provide helpful reading lists depending on your area of interest. Below are some non-technical general books and magazines that may be of interest to the concrete enthusiast.

Banham, Peter Reyner. *A Concrete Atlantis: US Industrial Buildings and European Modern Architecture 1900–1925* (Cambridge, Mass./London, MIT Press, 1986).

Banham, Peter Reyner. *The New Brutalism: Ethic or Aesthetic?* (London, Architectural Press, 1966).

Bennett, David. *Exploring Concrete Architeture: Tone, Texture, Form* (Basel, Birkhäuser, 2001).

Bennett, T P and Yerbury, F R. *Architectural Design in Concrete* (1927).

Collins, Peter. *Concrete: the Vision of a New Architecture. A Study of Auguste Perret and his Precursors* (London, Faber and Faber, 1959).

Escher, Frank, ed. *John Lautner Architect* (London, Artemis, 1994).

Hitchcock, Henry-Russell and Johnson, Philip. *The International Style: Architecture since 1922* (New York, MOMA, 1932).

Morris, A E J. *Precast Concrete in Architecture* (George Godwin, 1978).

Onderdonk, Dr Francis. *The Ferro-Concrete Style: Reinforced Concrete in Modern Architecture* (Santa Monica, Hennessey & Ingalls, 1998. First published 1928).

Building in Concrete 2000/1 (Munich, Atelier Kinold).

Slessor, Catherine. *Concrete Regionalism* (London, Thames & Hudson, 2000).

Stanley, C C and Bond, E G. *Concrete through the ages* (Crowthorne, British Cement Association, 1999).

ORGANIZATIONS

British Cement Association
Century House, Telford Avenue,
Crowthorne, Berkshire,
RG45 6YS, UK
www.bca.org.uk

Concrete Society
Postal address as above.
www.concrete.org.uk

British Precast Concrete Federation
60 Charles Street, Leicester,
LE1 1FB, UK
www.britishprecast.org.uk

Portland Cement Association
5420 Old Orchard Road
Skokie, Illinois 60077, USA
www. portcement.org

Concrete Association of Finland
PLII (Unioninkatu 14),
00 131 Helsinki, Finland
www.betoni.com

ACI American Concrete Institute
PO Box 9094, Farmington Hills,
Michigan 48333, USA
www.aci-int.net

Concrete Institute of Australia
PO Box 848, Crows Nest
Sydney, NSW 1585,
Australia
www.coninst.com.au

www.concretenetwork.com

LIST OF DESIGNERS

Emma Andrew, Marc Salamon / Apartment
171 Ashmore Road, London W9 3DA, UK

Ron Arad Associates
62 Chalk Farm Road, London NW1 8AN, UK

Peter Wylly / Babylon Design
301 Fulham Road, London SW10 9QH, UK

Eric Barrett
Arch 267, 241 Coldharbour Lane,
London SW9 8RR, UK

Kelvin Birk
Studio E3, Cockpit Arts, Cockpit Yard,
London WC1, UK

CVO Fire
36 Great Titchfield Street, London, UK

Kathy Dalwood
165 Victoria Road, London
NW6 6TE, UK

Field Day
30 Grove Place, London
NW3 1JR, UK

Tom Hurt Design
800 Christopher Street, Austin,
TX 78704, USA

Francesco Passaniti
Bétons Animés, 67 Rue Maurice
Gunsbourg, 94200 Ivry sur Seine, France

Retrouvious
32 York House, Upper Montague Street,
London W1H 1FR, UK

Rachel Reynolds / The Shed
121 Central Hill, London
SE19 1BY, UK

William Warren / WW Mod Cons
Units 2b & c, Vanguard Road, 36 Peckham
Road, London SE5 8QT, UK

Totem Design Ltd
2 Alexander Street, London W2 5NT, UK

Jesse Visser
Droog Design, Sarphatikade 11, 1017 Wv
Amsterdam, The Netherlands

Mark West
Faculty of Architecture
University of Manitoba, Winnipeg, MB,
RST 2N2, Canada

INDEX

AUTHOR'S ACKNOWLEDGMENTS

I would like to thank all those concrete enthusiasts out there who made this book possible; people who were rather surprised that a lay person was interested in concrete, but were happy to share information. Thanks to all those designers and architects who contributed to the book and demonstrate what a wealth of talent concrete has on its side.

The British Cement Association have been extremely supportive and their publication *Concrete through the Ages* was very helpful for piecing together the material's history. Martin Clarke supported the idea from the start and helped gain sponsorship. Thanks to Blue Circle whose sponsorship made the book possible.

I would also like to thank Piers Gough for his insightful foreword. Thanks also to Geri May for picture research, Amzie Viladot for his design and the editor, Jonathan Hilton. Also the dedicated team at Mitchell Beazley especially Mark Fletcher, who pushed the book when others thought concrete wasn't a worthy subject, Hannah Barnes-Murphy and Emily Asquith for doing a sterling job, being a pleasure to work with and becoming concrete enthusiasts in the process. Thanks to Claire Catterall, my partner at Scarlet Projects who indulged my concrete obsession, and lastly Dominic Papa who managed to listen to me going on about the wonders of concrete without getting prestressed and post-tensioned.

PICTURE ACKNOWLEDGMENTS

Tadao Ando Architect & Associates: photo Tadao Ando 116, photo Hiroshi Kobayashi 117, photo Mitsuo Matsuoka 129; Apartment: 106–7; Ron Arad Associates: 136–7; Arcaid: photo Richard Bryant 18, photo Nicholas Kane 88–9, photo Alan Weintraub back cover (top), 32–5, 43–5, 52–3, 59, 101, photo Ezra Stoller/Esto 69; Archipress: photo Luc Boegly 26–7, Klaus Frahm 126–7; Architectural Association: photo Sandra Denicke 20, 66–7; Babylon Design Ltd: photo Peter Wylly 83; Barragan Foundation: photo Armando Salas Portugal 122, 124–5; Eric Barrett 90–1; Kelvin Birk: 86–7; Block Architecture: photo Leon Chew 148–9; British Cement Association: endpapers, 9t & b, 16–17, 28, 100, 156–7, photo C Stanley 8; William P Bruder Architect Ltd: photo Bill Timmerman 150–1; Chinati Foundation: photo Todd Eberle 25; CVO Fire Products, courtesy Cool Blue 5, 92–3; CZWG Architects: photo Tim Street-Porter 104–5; Kathy Dalwood: 110–1; Denton Corker Marshall: photo Tim Griffith 48–51, 113; Droog Design: photo Marsel Loermans 94–5; Esto: photo Scott Frances 10, photo John Linden 29, Roberto Schezen 123, photo Ezra Stoller 70 ; Field Day: photo Bill Kingston 142–3; FOBA, Kyoto: photo Toshi Kobayashi 114–5; Olivier Hallot: 136–7; Tom Hurt Design: 118–9; IPC/Living Etc: photo Tim Young 128; JJ Photoservices: photo Trevor Jones 22; Rick Joy: 46–7; Knoll International: 97; Rem Koolhaas: photo Hans Werlemann 36–9; Adam Blackburne: photo Tom Manyon 85; Milliken, courtesy Direct Public Relations 24t; Minh+Wass Photography, New York: 108–9; Modcons: 140–1; The Modern Garden Company: photo Richard Brayshaw back cover (below), 72–3; Nobilis–Fontan: 24b; O'Donnell & Tuomey: photo John Searle 146–7; Jonathan Pile: 144–5; Premier Media Partners: photo Neil Davis 78–9; Royal Institute of British Architects: 11–12; Naoyuki Shirakawa: photo Fujitsuka Mitsumasa 62–3; The Shed: 80–1; Maria Speake: photos Nick Helm & Sean Cunningham 40–1; Margherita Spiluttini: architect Herzog & de Meuron 64–5, 98–9; Taverne Agency, Amsterdam: 54–7, photo Tom Bellard 130; Totem Design Ltd, London: 76–7, 140–1; United Net Studio, Amsterdam: photo Christian Richters 60–61; Rebecca Uth: front cover, 132–3; View: 15b, photo Phillip Bier 152.3, photo Peter Cook 13, 14t & b, 19t, 21, 68, 103, photo Chris Gascoigne 13, 23, photo Dennis Gilbert 31, 71, 131, photo Nick Meers 19b, photo Julie Phipps 15t; Carole Vincent: photo John Beswick 102; Mark West 75.